Mary Baker Eddy

Mary Baker Eddy

Discoverer and Founder of Christian Science

Louise A. Smith

The Christian Science Publishing Society
Boston, Massachusetts, U.S.A.

Contents

Introduction: Twentieth-Century Biographers Series

*I*N THE CLOSING YEARS
OF THE TWENTIETH CEN-
tury, there is a growing awareness that the hundred years
since 1900 will have registered a magnitude and pace of
change, in every aspect of human affairs, which probably
exceeds any historic precedent. In political, social and religious institutions and attitudes, in the sciences and industry,
in the arts, in how we communicate with each other,
humanity has traveled light years in this century.

"Earth's actors," said the Founder of Christian Science,
Mary Baker Eddy, "change earth's scenes...." As we look
back over the landscape of this century, some towering figures emerge into view: political leaders, scientists and inven-
tors, authors, artists and musicians, social and religious pioneers, industrialists, and many others who helped "change
earth's scenes."

Typically, when someone comes along who changes
human perceptions and ways of acting, he or she attracts

biographers. If an individual career is perceived, with growing distance, to have been especially significant in its impact
on human affairs and changing ideas, the shelf of biography
steadily expands; and each new published work, even
though it may cover some of the ground already treated in
earlier works, is expected to bring further insight into the
meaning of a life, a mind, and a career.

Even among those who are not her followers, Mary
Baker Eddy is customarily regarded as a major religious figure of the twentieth century and as a notable example of
the emergence of women in significant leadership roles. Her
works are visible today in virtually every country of the
world: in church buildings, in Christian Science Reading
Rooms, in the distribution of the newspaper and religious
periodicals she established and their derivative broadcast
forms, in the wide circulation of her own writings, and
most important, in the way hundreds of thousands of people conduct their everyday lives.

Public interest in Mrs. Eddy, and curiosity about her, are
as strong today as they were in 1910, the year of her
decease. And yet, compared with other major figures of the
century, the shelf of biography has increased little in the
intervening years. A handful of early biographies, by those
who knew her or stood close to her in time, were aug-
mented in the late 1960s by Robert Peel's monumental
three-volume work. Most of those early works, in spite of
their great value as part of the historical record, have lapsed
from print; and in fact some first-hand reminiscences by
individuals who worked directly with her have only been
privately published or circulated.

As we near the close of a century which directly wit-
nessed some of Mary Baker Eddy's major contributions, The

Christian Science Publishing Society, the publishing arm of the church she established, has reexamined the church's obligations to future generations and centuries, in providing an appreciation and understanding of her remarkable career.

Mrs. Eddy wrote only briefly about herself, in a short volume titled *Retrospection and Introspection.* She discouraged personal adulation or attention, clearly hoping that people would find her character and purpose in her own writings rather than in the biographic record. Yet, she came to see the need for an accurate account of her life and gave specific if possibly reluctant acquiescence in the year 1910 to the publishing of the first of the biographies — Sybil Wilbur's *Mary Baker Eddy.*

In addition to Robert Peel's trilogy, which is still in print, a number of significant biographic resources must remain, or become, permanently and readily available to future generations. These include: first-hand recollections of early workers who served directly under her leadership, not all of which have yet been published; and the various biographies which have already won their place in the history of Christian Science and in public use.

For these reasons, the Publishing Society welcomes the opportunity of publishing, and keeping in print, a major shelf of works on Mary Baker Eddy under the general series title: "Twentieth-Century Biographers Series."

Although a consistent set of editorial standards has been applied to such elements as indexing and footnoting, where required, with regard to dates, events, and statements of fact, the original texts of the authors have been preserved intact.

If the reader finds, through these volumes, occasional differing interpretations of events or concepts, this should serve as a strength rather than a weakness in a record which is so clearly synoptical in nature. Especially in the case of those who worked directly with Mrs. Eddy and shared many of her experiences, a special measure of respect and textual integrity is demanded. These are the workers she chose — individuals who served as her lieutenants, often for many years. To describe them as sturdy, strong-minded workers, patriarchal in their devotion and self-sacrifice, scarcely does them justice.

Mrs. Eddy's career and works have stirred humanity in the twentieth century and will continue to do so. Perhaps an appropriate introduction for this series is captured in her statement, in the Preface to *Science and Health with Key to the Scriptures*: "The time for thinkers has come." In that spirit, this series of biographies by many different twentieth-century writers, is offered to all those who, now and in the future, want to know more about this remarkable woman, her life and her work.

This volume, *Mary Baker Eddy, Discoverer and Founder of Christian Science,* has been written by a modern biographer. It is concurrently published by Chelsea House Publishers as part of their "American Women of Achievement" series. The "American Women of Achievement" series introduces fifty women "whose actions, ideas, and artistry have helped shape the course of American history." Included in the series are women such as Susan B. Anthony, Eleanor Roosevelt, Beverly Sills, and Mary Cassatt.

The Christian Science Publishing Society is pleased to include this book in its "Twentieth-Century Biographers Series."

Mary Baker Eddy

·M·B·E·

Mary Baker Eddy greets guests from the balcony of her Pleasant View estate in Concord, New Hampshire, in 1900. The founder and discoverer of Christian Science, Eddy lived quietly in her later years, away from the glare of publicity, but remained vitally involved with the church she led.

— 1 —

A Large Gathering

SUNDAY, JUNE 28, 1903,
HAD BEEN A MEANING-
ful day for those who were attending the Communion service of The First Church of Christ, Scientist, in Boston. The
city's newspapers were filled with accounts of the 3 services
held that day, which drew between 12,000 and 15,000
Christian Scientists. But late in the evening on June 28, the
Christian Scientists themselves were occupied with other
thoughts. Just hours before, a surprising invitation had been
received from their leader, Mary Baker Eddy, the founder
and discoverer of Christian Science. She invited the partici-
pants at the service, who had convened from all across the
United States and as far away as England, Germany, and
Australia, to visit the next day at her home, called Pleasant
View, outside Concord, New Hampshire.

Thousands of Christian Scientists immediately planned to
make the journey, for Eddy's personal appearances were
rare. Although she remained vitally interested in the affairs
of the church she had founded, she had retired from public activities more than a decade before in order to write
and pray. The multitude in Boston was eager to accept her

1

invitation, but transporting such a large number of people to Concord on such short notice was a daunting task in the days before automobiles. J. S. Smaus, one of Eddy's biographers, described in her book *Mary Baker Eddy: The Golden Days* how the church members busied themselves with preparations and the scene at Concord. Committees quickly formed and set to work: They contacted railroad officials, arranged special trains to Concord, and set about printing and issuing tickets.

Their preparations went smoothly, and throughout the next morning the special trains pulled into Concord one after another. The small city, the capital of New Hampshire, had prepared as well. Eddy was held in high esteem by Concord residents, and they did not hesitate to welcome the Christian Scientists. A private association, the Wonolancet Club, allowed the visitors to use its headquarters. The travelers from Boston thronged the streets. Smaus recounted the story told to her by a Concord resident who remembered how her sister as a young girl was "entranced at the sight of dignified Christian Science gentlemen in top hats sitting on the curb eating sandwiches out of a paper bag." Others ate lunch at the Wonolancet Club and were treated to lemonade and ice water.

The day was cool and pleasant, with an occasional drizzle of rain. Throughout the morning, Christian Scientists — some in horse-drawn carriages, others on foot — made the journey down Pleasant Street to Eddy's estate. By 1:00 P.M., approximately 10,000 people were waiting outside her closed street gates.

Eddy's remodeled farmhouse sat away from the road, surrounded by lawns, orchards, and gardens, where the household's vegetables were grown. Beyond the rear lawn and its ornamental pond lay a shallow river valley full of rolling meadows and woodlands; farther east, one could see the hills around the village of Bow, where Eddy was born 82 years before.

Eddy's birthplace was only a few miles away from her estate, but the path she had taken from Bow to Pleasant View had been long, involved, and filled with astonishing surprises. An editorial in the *Boston Journal* noted that thousands of people had traveled perhaps millions of miles to see Eddy out of "deep respect and tender love which has been awakened by one who, through God, has brought to unnumbered lives an unmeasured good."

Eddy's life and work had had a tremendous impact. An understanding of what drew so many to her home in New Hampshire is partially revealed in the expressions of affection, loyalty, and gratitude toward Eddy that had filled the days surrounding the annual meeting of Christian Scientists. The previous Saturday, the Executive Members of The Mother Church sent a dispatch to their "Beloved Teacher, Leader, and Guide":

> We desire on this occasion to reaffirm our implicit confidence in your leadership and guidance of our great cause, knowing as we do that you look to God in "all your ways." ...We congratulate you and all your adherents on the wonderful growth of the Christian Science movement under your wise and benign guidance, — a growth without parallel in the history of religion.

Hundreds testified at church meetings that they had been healed physically and spiritually through Christian Science, which Eddy had discovered in 1866 when she experienced a healing of serious injuries while reading the Bible. Thirteen years later, she founded the Church of Christ, Scientist, based on her understanding of the Bible.

The church's purpose, as recorded by Eddy in the *Manual of the Mother Church,* is to "commemorate the word and works of our Master [Jesus Christ], which should reinstate primitive Christianity and its lost element of healing."

According to Eddy, such healing results from attaining a true understanding of the nature of God and the world. It is not dependent on drugs or medical technology, and Christian Scientists do not ordinarily turn to medical doctors or study medical texts. Instead, the practice of Christian Science is based on prayer, spirituality, and close study of both the Bible and the Christian Science textbook, *Science and Health with Key to the Scriptures,* which was written by Eddy and initially printed in 1875.

Throughout the following years, Eddy toiled to make her teachings known. After many years of difficulties, Eddy finally saw the body of believers in Christian Science grow into a thriving church. By 1903, Eddy spent most of her days in seclusion, working in her study in a little tower on the back of the house. Her Christian Science lectures had once filled halls and classrooms. But following her own counsel, Eddy retired from active teaching to devote herself more fully to establishing the permanent organization of her church on a spiritual, rather than personal, basis.

Eddy believed that a church built on personality, even a personality as strong and authoritative as hers, was a church built on sand. She strove to base Christian Science on the "impersonal" — her written words — after seeing the instability of church activities that relied on personal charisma or even human goodness.

Under her written guidance, the church blossomed,

Books and papers lay piled high on a desk in Eddy's study at the back of Pleasant View. Eddy kept up with current events and maintained an extensive correspondence with Christian Scientists all over the world.

5

spreading throughout the world. She kept several corresponding secretaries busy sending out volumes of letters, addresses, and editorials. She continually revised *Science and Health* (which had reached its 261st printing in June 1903) and developed the By-Laws that governed the Church of Christ, Scientist. These By-Laws made up the *Manual of the Mother Church,* first published in 1895. Throughout the years, Eddy had written several other books as well as numerous articles for Christian Science periodicals.

Despite her productivity, disturbing rumors about her health circulated in several popular newspapers and magazines. Some journalists questioned whether Eddy was hiding from public view because she was an invalid, and they wondered if someone else was actually leading The First Church of Christ, Scientist. They openly accused her of being a charlatan and a fraud. To claim that the author of *Science and Health* was sick and infirm was a good way to undermine a growing movement — and a good way to sell newspapers.

Despite the animosity expressed by some members of the press, the spirit of the faithful outside Eddy's gates seemed to be one of quiet joy. The *Christian Science Sentinel* of July 4, 1903, recorded the events that followed. Shortly before 1:30 P.M., members of the Eddy household opened the gates and ushered the waiting guests onto the grounds. They walked in an orderly fashion, crowding near the east balcony outside of Eddy's study.

Eddy stepped out alone onto the balcony and paused to look upon the crowd, which became completely quiet. Many women silently waved handkerchiefs. The men took off their hats and, as a sign of respect, stood bareheaded. The light rainfall stopped.

Eddy wore an attractively trimmed purple wrap and an elaborate hat atop her short, curly gray hair. Very few wrinkles creased her face; observers frequently remarked that she looked like a woman half her age. She had large gray eyes that seemed to constantly deepen and change in color and intensity. She walked, erect as always, to the front of the balcony, folded her hands in front of her, and began to speak. As reported in the *Christian Science Sentinel,* her words were as follows:

"Beloved Brethren: — Welcome home! To your home in my heart! Welcome to Pleasant View, but not to varying views."

Her voice was clear and strong, so that her listeners later reported hearing each word. She spoke as she often instructed her students to, slowly and distinctly, as if they had something they wanted the world to hear.

She continued: "I would present a gift to you to-day, only that this gift is already yours. God hath given it to all mankind. It is His coin, His currency; it has His image and superscription. This gift is a passage of Scripture; it is my sacred motto, and it reads thus:

'Trust in the Lord, and do good; so shalt thou dwell in the land, and verily thou shalt be fed.' "

Eddy spoke for a moment longer and then smiled with obvious emotion at the listeners below. She waved good-bye several times before returning indoors to her study, her face radiantly happy.

Some students wept, and many scribbled down Eddy's

words. A few moments of silent prayer followed, and then, beginning with those nearest the balcony and spreading through the entire crowd, they sang one of her favorite hymns, "Shepherd, Show Me How to Go." As the hymn concluded, Eddy reappeared at the window, waving her handkerchief.

Several of Eddy's students recorded their memories of the day in the book *We Knew Mary Baker Eddy.* Mary Godfrey Parker, who stood under the balcony, said of the address, ". . . I felt as if I wanted to go off quietly by myself and just think about it."

Inside the study, John C. Lathrop, Eddy's corresponding secretary, listened to the address through the open window. When Eddy came back inside, her maid removed her hat and wrap. She sat down in the upholstered armchair that was the site of so many of her spiritual struggles. Lathrop also recounted the occasion in *We Knew Mary Baker Eddy.*

"Wasn't it a wonderful occasion," she said to Lathrop. Then she asked, "What are they doing?"

Lathrop looked out beyond the balcony and reported the gathering was praying silently.

"We will pray too," she said.

Outside, the 10,000 visitors sang the Communion hymn and the Doxology, said the Lord's Prayer, and then repeated one of the fundamental statements of Christian Science teaching, known as the scientific statement of being. The crowd began to disperse. Groups of two and three people walked together, quietly discussing Eddy's address.

When Lathrop told Eddy the crowd was leaving, she commented again on the beautiful occasion, "Now I will see what God says about it."

She picked up her Bible and, reaching out to God,

Eddy speaks to a throng of visitors gathered on her lawn
in 1900. Three years later an even larger crowd traveled
from the annual meeting of Christian Scientists in
Boston to Pleasant View at her invitation.

opened it randomly, as was her usual habit. The book fell open to the Old Testament, in the Book of Isaiah, chapter 35, verse 10. She read, "And the ransomed of the Lord shall return, and come to Zion with songs and everlasting joy upon their heads: they shall obtain joy and gladness, and sorrow and sighing shall flee away."

"See how God is always with me," she said. "That verse I will add to my address." She appended the verse to the end of the address's written version, which appeared in the July 4, 1903, *Christian Science Sentinel* and in her book *The First Church of Christ, Scientist, and Miscellany* (most often referred to simply as *Miscellany*).

Meanwhile, the household prepared for Eddy's regular afternoon carriage ride. There was a large staff living at Pleasant View. Virtually all of the jobs, such as maid, cook, laundress, and grounds keeper, were filled by Christian Scientists. Most were former students of Eddy's, chosen for their spiritual strength. The workers considered it a privilege to serve at Pleasant View, although some had trouble withstanding the demanding schedule for more than a few months.

As one of the household staff, Martha Wilcox, later recounted, Eddy required an orderly and efficient house: Mealtimes never varied, bed sheets were always turned down exactly two and one half inches, and each pin in her cushion was stuck in a particular corner according to its length. Eddy believed that being orderly and disciplined in day-to-day living helps in developing the Christian discipline needed to practice spiritual healing systematically.

Promptly at 2:00 P.M., Eddy settled into her carriage for the ride through Concord. The driver steered the horse-drawn carriage slowly between the crowds lining the paths.

All of the carriage windows were down. For most, this was the first and only time they would see their cherished leader up close. They shook handkerchiefs and bared their heads again as Eddy bowed repeatedly to the left and right.

This sight was a unique one for America: a living leader of her own religious denomination with a growing worldwide following. The struggle to ensure the survival of her church, however, would continue to be perilous.

"Millions may know that I am the Founder of Christian Science," she once wrote. "I alone know what that means."

Mark Baker looks forthrightly at the camera in a tintype (an early photograph). Mary's father was not only a farmer but also a stalwart member of the Congregational church and a highly esteemed citizen of Bow and Sanbornton Bridge. He performed several municipal duties, including that of coroner, justice of the peace, and trustee of the local academy.

— 2 —

A New Hampshire Childhood

*I*N BOW, NEW HAMP-
SHIRE, A SMALL FARM-
ing community nestled in the rolling hills along the Merrimack River, Mary Morse Baker was born on July 16, 1821.
In *Mary Baker Eddy: The Golden Days,* J. S. Smaus carefully
traced the Baker family history, and many details of Mary's
childhood are recorded in that book. Mary was the sixth
and last child of Mark Baker and Abigail Ambrose Baker.
Both her parents came from well-established New England
families: Mark was the youngest of 10 siblings; Abigail had
6 brothers and sisters. As a child, Mary sat on her grandmother Maryann Baker's knee and learned about her Scot-
tish and English ancestors who had come to the New
World and settled in New England seeking the "freedom to
worship God." She heard about her mother's father, who
was a deacon who paid for the building of the first Congregational church in Pembroke, New Hampshire, just
across the Merrimack River. Mark Baker grew up in Bow,
and when he married Abigail Ambrose, he brought her back
across on the Robinson ferry to make their home with his
mother on the Baker homestead.

Mark Baker was a tall, wiry farmer, whose picture shows a strong man with a firm jaw. Recollections from friends and family reveal him to have had an iron will and a capacity for measured kindness. Although he had received little formal schooling, the villagers often called him Squire Baker, referring to him by a title normally used for a rural judge or dignitary, because of the many services he provided to Bow and neighboring counties. Depending on the need of the moment, he helped out by occasionally performing the duties of a surveyor, a coroner, and a lawyer. Once, in a legal dispute between Bow and nearby Loudon, he argued the case for Bow against a successful young lawyer named Franklin Pierce and won. Franklin Pierce's father, Benjamin, was an acquaintance of Baker's. Twice elected governor of New Hampshire, Benjamin took an interest in some of the Baker children's fortunes later in life. His son Franklin eventually became the 14th president of the United States.

Baker certainly loved to argue politics, but as with many others of his day, nothing was more important to him than his religion. Smaus notes that while Mary was still an infant, Baker was elected to the post of clerk in the Union Church of Christ, the Congregational church his family attended. According to documents Smaus checked, his first duty as clerk was to record the Statements of Faith espoused by the congregation. They were firm assertions of orthodox Congregational tenets. Congregationalism had grown from the religion of the Puritans, the earliest English settlers in America, and their beliefs were drawn from the Protestant teachings of John Calvin, a 16th-century French theologian whose thought profoundly affected several Protestant denominations. The basic tenets of Calvinism included

Mary's birthplace and childhood home was a wooden house constructed in the saltbox style, popular in New England. Two stories in the front slope down to one story in the rear of the house, behind which lie a small extension and shed. A well for fresh water is shown in the far left foreground. Mary lived in this house with her parents, grandmother, and five brothers and sisters.

15

belief in God as all-knowing and all-powerful, belief in the total depravity of humankind, and belief in the divine grace offered by God to those few he elected to save from eternal damnation. This last belief is tied to Calvin's enormously influential doctrine of predestination — the idea that all humans are condemned to eternal hell except the small number God has marked for salvation. Mark Baker believed steadfastly in predestination and asserted his belief when talking with others concerned with the subject, including Abraham Burnham, the pastor of the Congregational church in nearby Pembroke, with whom he spent long hours discussing religion.

In contrast to her somewhat forbidding husband, Abigail reminded her friend, the Reverend R. S. Rust, of "the gentle dew and cheerful light." A short, round woman with blond hair and bright blue eyes, she too made religion the cornerstone of her family's life. Instead of stressing, as her husband did, that God was stern and unforgiving in meting out punishment to sinful humans, Abigail Baker taught her children to remember that their God was a loving God.

This emphasis on religion was by no means confined to the Bakers, whose daily life resembled that of most other early-19th-century New England farm dwellers. Although the atmosphere of the Baker home was suffused with religion, the days were filled with work. Wresting a living from their 200 acres of rocky land required constant effort. Mary's three oldest siblings were boys: Samuel, born in 1808; Albert, born in 1810; and George, born in 1812. They helped their father maintain the family almost entirely from their land — without the modern aids of electricity, running water, or power-driven machinery. Together they tilled the rocky soil, cultivating hay, grain, and vegetables. In their woodlot they grew, chopped, and piled the wood that warmed their small two-story home during the long, frigid New Hampshire winters. Their pastureland fed the eight oxen, five horses, three cows, and assorted other livestock that drew the plows and provided the family with milk, meat, and transportation. When their father settled the yearly accounts, they barely broke even, but the family never went hungry or lacked for necessities.

When Mary was born, her sister Abigail was five years old and her sister Martha was two and a half years old. When they were small, they watched Mary as an infant while she played indoors. Eventually, all three girls learned to help their mother with the myriad tasks of housekeeping on a farm. Abigail and her daughters not only cooked and cleaned but also preserved food, baked bread, made soap and candles, spun yarn, wove cloth, and sewed clothing for the family. However, in later years, as noted by Smaus, one of Mary's clearest memories was of sitting in a small rocker, looking at her Bible, in imitation of her mother and grandmother.

Mary later told one of her biographers, Irving S. Tomlinson, that her father "kept the family in the tightest harness I have ever known." Each day the clan assembled on benches for long, solemn prayers in the morning and evening. The prayer session included reading a chapter from the Bible and listening to a sermon from her father. Of her father, she later wrote, "I have never seen one who had such a gift of audible prayer." Her mother, on the other hand, did not speak at these sessions, as women of her era were expected to keep silent and yield to their husband.

Observance of the Sunday Sabbath, the biblical day of rest, was strictly enforced. "The children were not allowed to go elsewhere than to church — not even to the ceme-

tery," Mary later recalled. Between the morning and afternoon services they sat quietly with their hands folded on
their lap.

The year she turned five, Mary attended the summer session at the one-room schoolhouse a mile from the farm,
which had been built from a plan drawn up by Mark
Baker. All of the grades were taught in one room, and
Mary sat in the middle of the smaller benches in front,
where her feet could reach the floor.

Smaus records how Martha and Abigail, who sat behind
Mary, decided to show off their pretty and precocious sister
at lunchtime. Mary was already reading and, because of her
excellent memory, often served as the family prompter,
reminding them of conversations and sermons everyone else
had long since forgotten. In the school yard, Martha and
Abigail sat Mary on a table and asked her what she wanted
to be when she grew up. The other children crowded
around.

"When I grow up, I want to write a book!" Mary
replied. The schoolchildren laughed about her unique
answer. Most of them, as Smaus notes, probably would have
replied they wanted to be a mother or a farmer.

Mary planned to study hard to reach her goal but ill
health frequently kept her out of school. Fevers, backaches,
and dyspepsia (persistent digestive problems) sent her to bed
for long stretches of time. Her father believed she made
herself sick by reading too much. One doctor, with whom
her father largely concurred, recommended, "Do not doctor
your child, she has got too much brains for her body; keep
her out of doors, keep her in exercise, and keep her away
from school all you can."

The Bakers cared for their children's spiritual well-being

as well as for their physical needs. Mary's mother often instructed the children at bedtime. She repeated such maxims as, "It is more blessed to give than receive." With her youngest daughter, she learned to lighten the lessons because Mary took these rules quite literally. In *Mary Baker Eddy: The Golden Days,* several particularly revealing stories about Mary are told, including the following one. At school, Mary would give away her mittens, scarf, and coat if a poorly clad classmate shivered in the cold. Mary insisted she could not ignore someone in distress, but her mother eventually began to remind her as she dressed her for school, "You must not give away your clothes. Mother does not have time to make others."

Mary's cheerful and kind disposition made her the family favorite. They spoiled her just as she spoiled the small farm animals when they were sick, nursing them back to health. Despite her charm, she could also be as stubborn as her father and often stood up to him. Baker would hide Mary's books, but Mary would find them. When she did attend school, she slept with her schoolbook under her pillow.

Schools in New Hampshire in the 1820s differed greatly from modern schools. The availability of schoolbooks in Mary's day was quite limited, and students were expected to learn by memorization and repetition. Mary practically memorized the Lindley Murray *Grammar* and learned by heart the Westminster Catechism, a statement of Protestant beliefs. She also read the Lindley Murray *Introduction to the English Reader* and *The English Reader,* long collections of poetry and prose from adult writers of a century before, such as Joseph Addison, Alexander Pope, and Oliver Goldsmith. Their complicated sentences and difficult vocabulary could be daunting to a child, but Mary and her siblings made their way through them.

One of her brothers in particular excelled at academics. Albert was determined to go to college and worked as a teacher to make the money he needed to do so. He taught primary school for a semester in the town of Concord, New Hampshire, and another term in the school that his brothers and sisters attended. Finally, he had enough money to attend Dartmouth College, and the summer he returned home after his freshman year, Mary's world of scholarship truly opened wide. Although Albert was 11 years older than Mary, both shared a love of knowledge, and she later wrote that he was "next to my mother, the very dearest of my kindred."

Albert was considered to be the Baker child with the best chance of a brilliant career. Not only was he intelligent, but he was also attractive and charming. He had a beautiful tenor voice, Mary recalled, and she told Tomlinson, "people would come miles to hear him sing." Mary worked hard to earn her brother's pride. Albert even taught her a bit of Hebrew, Greek, and Latin during the summers. They talked of how she could become a writer, and Mary declared, "I must be as great a scholar as you or Mr. Franklin Pierce." (The younger Pierce was highly regarded for his abilities.)

At the age of 12, Mary began ambitiously modeling verses after the popular poetry she read in newspapers and magazines. One poem she called "Resolutions for the Day." Its last stanza ran as follows:

> If these resolutions are acted up to,
>   And faith spreads her pinions abroad,
> 'Twill be sweet when I ponder the days may be few
>   That waft me away to my God.

Mary continually struggled with her conception of God. From her earliest years she recalled listening to her father argue about predestination with her older cousin in the kitchen as she lay awake in her trundle bed in the next room. She always "wanted to know who won," and then she reviewed the discussion long into the night.

Eddy later wrote that when she was 12 years old, one day she asked her mother if she thought such a thing as eternal punishment could really be true.

"Mary, I suppose it *is*," her mother replied.

Mary thought a moment and replied, "What if we repent and tell God 'we are sorry and will not do so again' — will God punish us? Then He is not as good as my mother and He will find me a hard case."

Mary occasionally argued with her father about such beliefs, and her outbursts sometimes put the Baker home in an uproar, as Smaus reports. Her mother and sisters usually sided with Mary, and her father once concluded, "The Bible says Mary Magdalene had seven devils but our Mary has got ten!"

In her memoir, *Retrospection and Introspection,* Mary recalled the outcome of a particularly tumultuous discussion of predestination. She became so distressed that she developed a high fever. As her mother cooled her with wet cloths, she reminded Mary to lean on God's love and seek his guidance. Mary prayed and eventually a feeling of joy spread through her. She wrote, "The fever was gone, and I rose and dressed myself, in a normal condition of health. Mother saw this, and was glad. The physician marvelled; and the 'horrible decree' of predestination — as John Calvin rightly called his own tenet — forever lost its power over me."

As Mary grew older, more than her views on predestination altered. Her brothers and sisters took varying paths from the Baker household. Her eldest brother, Samuel, had gone to Boston years earlier to enter the construction business and had married Eliza Glover, a sister of his coworker George Washington Glover, in March 1832; in 1833, Samuel and Eliza had a son. (Samuel's wedding remained vivid in Mary's memory, for during the reception, George Washington Glover had set her on his knee and claimed he would later marry her.) The following year, when Mary turned 13, was even more eventful for her family. In the spring of 1834, her beloved brother Albert graduated from Dartmouth College and was invited to stay with the Pierces in their imposing home, where he studied law. Within a year, in January 1835, Mary's grandmother Baker died, and a few months later, Mary's brother George Sullivan Baker left the family farm and set off to make his way in Connecticut. Mary's older sister Abigail also went to live with the Pierces that year and began teaching school. Chatty letters filled with news and daily events flew back and forth and took the place of talks among the siblings by the fireplace. Only four Bakers remained at home on the farm at Bow — Mary, her sister Martha, and their parents. Soon, even that circumstance would change.

After the death of his mother, Mark Baker felt less tied to the Baker homestead. He decided to sell the old family farm and buy another. Robert Peel wrote of how Baker decided where to move. His brother Philip had discovered a pleasant piece of land about 20 miles to the north of Bow and promptly bought it; Mark liked Philip's new land and found acreage that satisfied him nearby. Both farms were just outside the town of Sanbornton Bridge, and Mark eagerly started preparations to move.

A woodcut portrays the village of Sanbornton Bridge on the banks of the Winnepesaukee River. The Bakers moved to a farm on the outskirts of Sanbornton in 1836, and the Baker girls proved popular residents of the rapidly growing town.

23

Mary, about to lose her childhood home, did not share her father's enthusiasm. When the family was about to depart, she fell ill, as did her mother, and the Bakers could not settle into their new home until the beginning of 1836. When Mary was well enough to make the 22-mile trip, she wrote a poetic good-bye to her friend and neighbor Andrew Gault:

> Hard is the task to take a final leave
> Of friends whom we shall see ah! never
> With unaccustomed grief my bosom heaves
> And burns with latent fire forever.

Abigail and Mary's misgivings proved unfounded, for Sanbornton Bridge turned out to be a congenial spot for the Bakers. Several textile mills and factories, part of the Industrial Revolution that was sweeping New England, had sprung up there and flourished in the village. The family settled into the community, and the girls soon discovered the town had a lively social life. Abigail returned home after her term as teacher finished and plunged into a whirl of visits. Before long, the Baker girls' letters to their brothers were filled with news of new friends, intellectual conversations in the evenings, gentlemen callers, and parties. (Mark Baker kept careful watch over his daughters, however. Peel recorded that Baker greeted male callers with the injunction, "Let all conversation and pleasure be in harmony with the will of God," and did not let his daughters attend dances.)

By the time summer arrived, Mary had grown strong enough to attend the whole summer term of school that year. She quickly became one of the town belles, with her thick eyelashes and wavy brown hair. A cousin later recalled her "transparent skin & brilliant blue eyes," and other con-

Academy Hall housed the Woodman Sanbornton Academy, which Mary attended in the early 1840s. She took every opportunity to continue her formal education.

temporaries noted her charm and liveliness. In the rough-hewn mill town, she and her sisters stood out with their refined manners and dress. Mary delighted in keeping up-to-date and followed changing fashions closely.

Once she was too old to study at the village school, she attended the local academies sporadically when she was well enough and her family had enough ready cash to pay the tuition. (There were no public high schools, but a number of private schools existed.) Although school records are sketchy, Peel and Smaus agree that Mary probably attended the Woodman Sanbornton Academy sometime between her arrival in 1836 and 1842. Her favorite studies at the time were natural philosophy, logic, and moral science. Her sister Martha probably attended classes with her, but Abigail's school days were over. In July 1837, she became Abigail Tilton when she married Alexander Hamilton Tilton, the wealthy owner of several mills in Sanbornton Bridge. That same month, Albert Baker passed the bar, qualifying him to practice law, much to the pride of his family, especially his youngest sister.

Mindful of Albert's example, Mary applied herself to academics when she was able. At the same time, she did not neglect religion. In July 1838, she joined the Congregational church in the town a few weeks after her parents became members. Several biographers recorded that her admittance to the church was not without trouble, for she still struggled against accepting the doctrine of predestination. The doctrine that all who did not join the church were indubitably damned horrified her, for she was the first of the Baker children to become a member of the congregation. In later life she recalled that the minister "would not let me enter into the church unless I believed in foreordination

The white clapboard Congregational church at Sanbornton Bridge was typical of the steepled churches that dotted the New England countryside and were centers of community life there. Mary joined the Sanbornton Congregational church in 1838, when she was 17.

[predestination], and I told him I would not be saved and my brothers and sisters have no chance. I was made sick by it, because I could not believe in it, and I stood out and would not join the church and the old man gave in and took me in," adding, "and my protest along with me."

At 17, she taught Sunday school to the youngest children in her church. One of her students told biographer Sibyl Wilbur, "She always wore clothes we admired. We liked her gloves and fine cambric handkerchief. She was, as I have come to understand, exquisite, and we loved her particularly for her daintiness, her high bred manners, her way of smiling at us."

True to her nature, however, Mary was interested in more than just fashion. She noticed that Lyman Durgin, the Bakers' orphaned stableboy, was not attending Sunday school. She questioned him at home and discovered he was embarrassed because he could not read well and so was unable to memorize and recite Bible verses as the others did. Mary set to work tutoring Lyman. She read the New Testament out loud to him, and he memorized her words. Soon, he was attending Sunday school, although Mary continued to tutor him for four years.

Lyman remained devoted to Mary throughout their youth and rode to fetch the doctor for her on many a frigid night. A variety of ailments plagued both her and Martha, although Mary's troubles appear to have been more serious. Throughout her brothers' and sisters' letters are scattered references to her health. Peel noted some of their comments. In 1837, Abigail wrote, "...the poor girl can never enjoy life as most of us can should she live any time, and this is altogether uncertain." Albert was particularly solicitous, for he remained close to Mary, although his increasingly successful career took him far from Sanbornton Bridge. He noted in an 1840 letter to Martha and Mary: "I know there is *honesty* and *sincerity* in a sister's love. But my joy was saddened, upon reading in your postscript, that Mary's health is again in danger." But it was not Mary's ill health that would cut short his promising career.

Through the newspapers and his letters home, Mary followed Albert's rise through the political ranks. He was her closest connection to the affairs of the larger world away from Sanbornton Bridge. After only two years as a successful lawyer, part of which included managing Franklin Pierce's practice when Pierce became a U.S. senator, Albert was elected to the New Hampshire state legislature in 1839. He was largely responsible for a new law prohibiting imprisonment for debt. Later, he was encouraged to run for Congress, but before the congressional election, Albert died on October 17, 1841, at the age of 31, of a kidney ailment.

Stunned by the loss of her favorite brother, Mary Baker began an adulthood that would continue to grow much darker before she found light.

One of the earliest known pictures of Mary Baker Glover is
this tintype, probably taken in the late 1840s. The period
was a troubled one for her; as a young widow, she was
left nearly destitute to care for an infant son while she
suffered greatly from a variety of illnesses.

— 3 —

"What Is Left of Earth to Me!"

ARY BAKER WROTE A POEM IN 1841 IN which she expressed the fear that her life would amount to nothing. She was 20 years old and before long would be the last child left in her parents' home. Abigail was married, Martha was engaged, and Albert was gone forever. Mary despaired, musing on the thought that she too might die young, but unlike her brother, she would leave no accomplishment worth remembering.

Her character and spirit did not allow her to wallow in grief and confusion, however. Smaus and Peel noted that she remained close to her circle of friends, which included Augusta Holmes, Martha "Mathy" Rand, and Hannah Sanborn, and as a result of another connection, Baker soon had several publications to her credit. One of her former teachers at the Woodman Sanbornton Academy, Sarah Bodwell, had praised her literary efforts and eventually became a friend. In 1841, Bodwell married Charles Lane, who published the *Belknap Gazette,* and as a result, several of

Baker's poems appeared in print there. In addition, others were published in the *New Hampshire Patriot and State Gazette.*

Some of her literary efforts were meant for an audience of one. George Washington "Wash" Glover, who had long ago announced, perhaps jokingly, that Mary Baker would be his bride, became more serious as time went on. He had begun corresponding with her several years before and although he moved to Charleston, South Carolina, he managed to visit Sanbornton Bridge in the summer of 1841, according to Smaus. The two young people then stepped up the pace of their correspondence, and as Baker recalled to Tomlinson many years later, ". . . in this way we got acquainted, for in writing to him I became very fond of him."

News of romance, weddings, and engagements filled the Baker household. In late 1842, both Baker's sister Martha and Baker's friend Augusta Holmes were married. Martha chose Luther Pilsbury, the brother of Amos Pilsbury, with whom George Baker had worked in Connecticut, and the couple moved to Concord. Augusta married a close friend of Albert's, Samuel Swasey, and they settled in Haverhill, New Hampshire. Although Baker mentioned a number of young men, including John Bartlett, an old friend, in her letters to Martha and Augusta, she did not neglect Wash Glover in faraway South Carolina. He faithfully reciprocated until, to Baker's dismay, his letters abruptly stopped in early 1843. Smaus told the story of what happened next.

Baker imagined the worst, but her brother George, who had returned to Sanbornton and joined Alexander Tilton at his mill enterprises, suspected a reason closer to home — that their father had been intercepting the letters. George

A portrait believed to be that of George Washington Glover is preserved in the Longyear Museum and Historical Society. Glover was a friend and business associate of Samuel Baker, and contemporary accounts reveal him to have been a handsome, outgoing young man with a successful building business. He and Mary Baker were wed in 1843.

guessed that perhaps Mark Baker, seeing Mary's friend and his daughter Martha so recently married, thought that Mary would be next and feared that if she chose Glover, she would go much farther than Concord or Haverhill. But George viewed the match in a different light. He thought highly of his old friend and just two years earlier had received a letter from Glover, boasting that he was doing half of all the building in Charleston. Despite this news of Glover's success, as far as Mark and Abigail Baker were concerned, he was not an ideal suitor. South Carolina was so distant it might as well as have been a different nation. Mark wanted only to protect Mary, but her obvious unhappiness moved George to take action. He suggested that she go with him on a business trip to the White Mountains; meanwhile, he told Glover of their route and the hotel stops their stagecoach would make.

George was right; Glover's letters caught up to Mary in the mountains. Mary was delighted to find that her fears were groundless and enjoyed a pleasant visit with Augusta at Haverhill along the way. Mary returned happily to Sanbornton Bridge, and sometime during the summer and fall, her parents finally acquiesced to her eventual departure as Glover's bride. Joyfully, the young couple made wedding plans for the end of the year.

On Sunday, December 10, 1843, Mary Baker wedded George Glover in her father's parlor; later she wrote, "I married young the one I loved." Her new husband was a tall, outgoing man with plenty of energy. He had arrived in South Carolina in 1838 and within five years had a host of friends and a thriving business. Peel records that together the newlyweds traveled to Concord, made a brief trip to Mary's childhood home of Bow, and took the train — an innovation that had begun operation only three years before — to Boston, where they embarked on a ship south.

After a stormy voyage, during which the new Mrs. Glover was "hopelessly seasick," she gazed with delight on the wide magnolia-lined streets and elegant buildings of Charleston. The Glovers spent only a month or so in Charleston, for George had business in the town of Wilmington, apparently connected with his latest building project, the construction of a cathedral in Haiti, an island-nation in the Caribbean. In both Charleston and Wilmington, George had many friends and business acquaintances, for he was an active member of several fraternal groups, including the Masonic order and the Independent Order of Odd Fellows (I.O.O.F.). Dinner parties, pleasure trips with new friends, and evenings at the theater kept Mrs. Glover busy. Peel uncovered the reminiscences of several of her acquaintances. One Wilmington resident recalled that Mrs. Glover was "a very beautiful woman, brilliant in conversation, and most gracious in her manner." Harriet Brown, the daughter of another contemporary, remarked, "She was extremely beautiful, one of the prettiest young women I have ever seen."

Despite the social whirl, Glover did not abandon her literary interests. Harriet Brown also remembered, "I imagine that she was always great for writing verses, for she had no sooner come to Wilmington than she began contributing rhymes to the local paper." The newlywed also saw several of her works appear in a new publication called *Heriot's Magazine: The Floral Wreath & Ladies Monthly Magazine* and was invited to write toasts for a Democratic party dinner.

In June, tragedy ended the southern idyll. Glover's store of building materials for the Haitian cathedral, into which he had sunk almost all his money, was destroyed. Peel noted that in later years, Mary could not remember whether they were stolen or burned, probably because a few days later the disaster was overshadowed by an even greater one. Glover contracted a fatal case of yellow fever, and his wife, six months pregnant at the time, was widowed on June 27, 1844. George Washington Glover's funeral was held the following day.

Members of the Masonic order kindly helped the young widow, but there was no reason for her to remain in South Carolina. Mary Glover's money was gone; she had no family in the South. One of her friends in the Masons traveled with her on the long, sad journey north to her parents' home. According to Peel, the rigorous four-day trek included riding on four different trains, passages on five steamboats and a ferry, two carriage trips, and a night in New York City. The heat and discomfort were intense.

Glover's parents welcomed their grieving daughter. She moved into her old room in her parents' house and gave birth to George, Jr., on September 12, 1844. The calamities of the summer, the rigors of the trip north, and Glover's continuing poor health made the delivery difficult and apparently injured her. Glover was unable to care for her newborn son, so the infant was taken to a woman who could nurse him, as was usual in such cases in those days. Childbirth was frequently difficult. Nine months later Mary's sister Abigail gave birth to a son, Albert, and her health was also precarious. However, Abigail recovered more quickly than her sister. Glover slowly improved but remained too weak to take care of a boisterous, active toddler. Mahala Sanborn, the family nurse, took over most of the responsibility for George, Jr., when Glover could not handle him.

As she regained her strength, Glover searched for a means to support herself and her young son. Like most women of her century, she was trained to do little. Poorer women could work in the mills as unskilled factory laborers, but Glover's social standing and health made such a course inconceivable. One of the only professions open to educated 19th-century women was teaching, and Glover soon learned that her old friend Mathy Rand had taken this path and was teaching in the village school. (Smaus recorded that George Baker, who had gained prominence in Sanbornton and was a member of the district school committee, commended her work particularly warmly.) But Rand soon quit her job to take classes at the educational institution that replaced the old Sanbornton Academy, the New Hampshire Conference Seminary, where Reverend R. S. Rust was principal. Peel noted that Rust joined George Baker, Mathy Rand, and John Bartlett in the circle of Glover's close friends. He noticed Glover's natural teaching abilities and suggested that she open a primary school for young children.

Eager to aid the impoverished young widow, Abigail and Alexander Tilton decided that a small building on their land was perfect for Glover to use. They hired painters to give it a fresh coat of red paint and outfitted it with tables and chairs especially sized for younger children. Although the Baker children had attended school when they were young, they went only during the summer, when most of their older siblings were away from class at work on the farm, and even then children of several ages were mixed in one class. Glover's primary school opened in 1846 as one of the first of its kind in New England. It was akin to a kindergarten of today, but in the 19th century such a school was a startling innovation.

Glover demonstrated an uncanny ability to elicit her pupils' best behavior. She later explained her disciplinary method: "The way to have children stop doing wrong is to have them love to do right." Her original ways proved to be too much for the conservative parents of Sanbornton. The school met with criticism, Glover's health remained delicate, and George demanded her attention. The experiment eventually failed.

Glover turned again to writing and spent much of 1847 composing with little George at her elbow. Isaac Hill, known as the Democratic dictator of New Hampshire, invited her to comment on political issues, especially slavery, in his newspaper, *Hill's Patriot,* and she contributed to the *I.O.O.F. Covenant* and *Freemason's Weekly* as well. The growing interest in the western territories even inspired her to write a novelette, *Emma Clinton, A Tale of the Frontier.* However, her writing income was not substantial.

Although Glover was a widow with a son, she was only 26 years old and received a great deal of attention from the town's single men. The townspeople gossiped mightily about the suitors' comings and goings. When John Bartlett left for his last year at Harvard Law School, Glover wrote her friend Mathy Rand of her relief that the neighbors would now "mind their business about either of us, as I am getting a little *mad* at their *lies,* for such they are."

Eventually, Bartlett and Glover did grow quite close, and as Peel discovered, she went to Cambridge, Massachusetts, to attend his graduation late in the summer of 1848. Her mother noted in a letter to George Baker, who had moved to New York, that Glover had made up her mind. But in 1849, Bartlett decided to travel west. California, where the gold rush had just exploded, seemed to offer greater opportunities than old New England. They agreed to marry upon his return home or when she could join him in the West.

Plans for many changes were under way. George Baker became engaged to Mathy Rand. While Glover was in Warner, New Hampshire, where she was sent for two months of treatment after her health worsened, her father made plans to move into a larger house in Sanbornton Bridge. However, that fall brought tragedy along with joy. George did return early in November and wedded Mathy; together they immediately moved to Baltimore, Maryland. Within the month, Mary Glover's mother, Abigail Ambrose Baker, passed away, and only weeks later a letter arrived from Sacramento announcing Bartlett's death there.

"What is left of earth to *me!*" Glover wrote to her brother George. In another year, there was to be even less. Glover suffered from recurrent illness, requiring six-year-old George Glover to spend an increasing amount of time with Mahala Sanborn in the Sanborn family home. Martha's husband, Luther Pilsbury, had died in October 1850 on a trip to Illinois, and Mark Baker had two widowed daughters and three fatherless grandchildren on his hands. When he remarried in December 1850, he realized he could not continue to provide a home for them all. Martha went to stay with her Pilsbury relatives, but Mark could not take care of both his daughter and his grandson. Glover was not sure that she wanted to stay with her father in any case, for when her new stepmother's "best carpets and goods" arrived, her father expected her to help arrange them in place of her deceased mother's furniture. ". . . I will see them in the bottomless pit before doing it," she wrote.

In this difficult situation, Abigail Tilton opened her home to her sister — but on one condition: She could not bring George with her. As Smaus noted, Tilton felt that the rambunctious George was too much of a strain on her son Albert's health as well as on her own and Glover's. When Mahala Sanborn married Russell Cheney and planned to move 40 miles upstate to North Groton, New Hampshire, Tilton arranged for the Cheneys to take George with them. The night before George left, Glover wept over each of his garments. She later wrote in her autobiography that she "knelt by his side throughout the dark hours, hoping for a vision of relief from this trial." Peel noted that a poem she jotted in her journal on May 9, 1851, the day after George left, reveals her anguish. In it, she spoke of a "Mother's voiceless woe/Too keen for utterance, too deep for tears!"

George's high spirits may have been too much for Glover to handle, but apparently George's absence was more than she could bear. Her health grew even worse. In January 1852, Mathy Rand Baker received a letter from Martha Pilsbury in which she confided, ". . . there is scarcely a ray of hope left us of her [Glover's] recovery. Her strength gradually fails, and all the powers of life seem yielding to the force of disease."

Gradually, her spells of good health became longer. She remained an attractive woman, still interested in fashion and intellectual pursuits. The answer to Glover's dilemma seemed to appear in the person of a suitor — Dr. Daniel Patterson, a dentist who treated her for a toothache. The two corresponded afterward, and they were married in June 1853. Although she later wrote in her autobiography, "My dominant thought in marrying again was to get back my

Daniel Patterson, a traveling dentist, married Mary Baker Glover
in 1853. The couple moved north to Franklin, New Hampshire,
and then to North Groton, where Mary Patterson hoped to
spend time with her son, who had been sent there to
live with the Cheney family.

child," she did find Patterson's hearty manner genuinely appealing, and Peel noted that their letters to each other reveal real affection.

The Pattersons moved to a house in Franklin, New Hampshire. He had promised to make a place in their home for George Glover but changed his mind when his wife's health continued to be unstable — as did his finances. Mary Patterson was alone in the house much of the time, far from her son and family. She wrote to her sisters, expressing her low spirits, but they had troubles of their own. The Tiltons were coping with the effects of a disastrous fire in their mill and could not help. Eventually, Dr. Patterson borrowed money from Martha Pilsbury and bought property, a house, and part of a sawmill in North Groton, where his wife hoped to see her son, who lived there with the Cheneys. One of the Cheneys' nieces later recalled that the isolated spot was particularly bad for Dr. Patterson's practice.

North Groton did not prove to be good for his wife either. Much as Patterson wished to be with her son, Smaus noted that reports of the boy's conduct alarmed Dr. Patterson and he would not let the two see each other. George had grown up roughly, for the Cheneys did not think much of schooling and did not care whether or not he attended classes. They not only neglected his education but also failed to discipline him, and Dr. Patterson neither liked the boy nor thought him fit to see his mother. Then in April 1856, without Mary Patterson's knowledge, the Cheneys joined the great westward migration of Americans and took George with them to Minnesota.

Mary was so devastated that she became extremely ill. Dr. Patterson was unable to support his household by work in North Groton, and he roamed the countryside for long

The Pattersons' house in Franklin, New Hampshire. Mary
Patterson endured continuing difficulties despite her marriage and
change of residence — she and her son remained apart, her
debilitating spells of illness persisted, and her husband
spent long periods of time away from home.

periods of time, leaving his wife confined to bed with a blind girl to care for her. She wrote and read. To her friend Mathy Rand Baker, she noted that she was "so weary of solitude I have half determined this very moment to throw aside my pen and wait to *weep."*

In the mornings, Patterson's attendant, Myra Wilson, lifted her into a chair and rolled her onto the porch, where she could breathe in the mountain air. Patterson spent much time reading the Bible, always a solace to her, and entertained visitors when she was able. Fond of children, she helped several with their studies. When they were adults, several North Groton residents remembered with great affection her kindnesses to them in their younger days, and one commented that she was "a lover of children and in return all children loved her." Some delighted in bringing berries and flowers to "the good sick lady."

Mary Patterson had several medical problems but seems to have received only minimal relief from the treatments then popular. At the time, doctors had little comprehension of the causes of disease. During the first half of the 19th century, they relied on bloodletting, purging the patient, and administering doses of whatever medication was in vogue, including several potentially harmful drugs, such as morphine. In response to such drastic, often fatal, measures, the public turned to a wide range of alternative practices.

Patterson herself experimented with cures. An intelligent, spirited woman, she was determined to help herself. She tried eating only coarse bread and vegetables. She also read with great interest the advertisements for home remedies and unusual cures that filled the newspapers of the day and "studied a large Doctor's book on homeopathy," as Wilson later recalled.

Homeopathy, a system of medical treatment founded by

Samuel Hahnemann, was extremely popular in the 19th century. A homeopath treats a sick person by administering minute quantities of a drug that, if given to a healthy person, would produce the symptoms of the disease from which the patient suffers. Anyone who carefully studies the diagnoses and prescriptions in the books written by Hahnemann and his followers can practice the system. Patterson was greatly interested in homeopathy during this period, and "neighbors would come occasionally for medicine which she would give them," Wilson recalled.

Patterson, however, became increasingly convinced that a person's mind controlled the body's sickness and health. As Peel noted, the particular tenet of homeopathy that led her to this conclusion was "the law of the minimal dose" — Hahnemann's thesis that the smaller the dose the more effective the remedy. One particular experience that she recorded in *Science and Health* strengthened this idea. A woman visited her who suffered from dropsy (excess accumulation of water in the body). Patterson prescribed a very diluted homeopathic drug for the condition, but eventually, without the woman's knowledge, she replaced the drug with unmedicated sugar pellets. The woman continued to improve, except on the days Patterson withheld the pellets. In an interview many years later, Patterson compared her conclusions about the woman's complete recovery with the fanciful tale of how Isaac Newton thought of the theory of gravity when an apple dropped from a tree onto his head. The woman's recovery "was a falling apple to me — it made plain to me that mind governed the whole question of her recovery."

Patterson sought earnestly for answers about the ills of the body but never neglected spiritual matters. She always took advantage of her spells of health by attending the

Congregational church in North Groton, and in *Retrospection and Introspection* she wrote of her effort "to seek diligently for the knowledge of God as the one great and ever-present relief from human woe." More woes were soon to come.

Dr. Patterson's practice was doing poorly, and he found himself unable to repay the money Martha Pilsbury had lent him for the North Groton house. On her part, she did not want to foreclose on the mortgage and sell the property, but her financial situation allowed no other course. In March 1860, an auction was held and Mrs. Patterson had to leave her home. Her sister Abigail brought her to a rooming house in the nearby village of Rumney, where she stayed awaiting her husband's return. She remained in a poor state of health. Finally, he managed to install her in a house in Rumney, but another calamity awaited.

The Civil War broke out in 1861. The tragic war did, however, occasion one event that brought her great joy — she received a letter from her son on October 10, 1861. It was the first communication she had received from him in more than five years. George Glover, high spirited as ever, had run away from the Cheneys at the age of 17 and enlisted in the Union army. There, as Peel wrote, he met David Hall, a man who specialized in writing letters for soldiers who could not write for themselves. Somehow, at George's request, Hall obtained Mrs. Patterson's address, and George happily dictated a letter to his long-lost mother. He continued to send her regular missives.

Patterson found comfort in these letters, for once again she was alone and ill. Dr. Patterson tried to do his part for the Union and in 1862 undertook a mission from the governor of New Hampshire that involved traveling to Washington, D.C. While observing the battle lines at nearby Bull

Run, he was captured by the Confederate army and thrown in prison. His capture, on top of Patterson's worsening health, left her in serious straits. Once again, her family rallied to help her.

Her sisters and brothers, like Dr. Patterson, must occasionally have found her spells of ill health exasperating, but all of them made efforts to find effective treatment for her. During 1861, the Pattersons evidently inquired about two different types of cures. Before traveling to the South, Dr. Patterson sent a letter to Phineas P. Quimby, a practitioner in Portland, Maine, who was reputed to have great success with his system of "mind cure." At the time, though, Quimby could not visit New Hampshire. Mrs. Patterson had also written to Dr. W. T. Vail's Hydropathic Institute, an establishment in Hill, New Hampshire, and asked about boarding near the institute. While Dr. Patterson was imprisoned in the South, Mary wrote to her sister Abigail, asking for the money to visit Quimby for treatment. Tilton refused to enable her to consult a man who professed such an unusual method of healing. She did, however, pay for Patterson's extended visit to Vail's Hydropathic Institute, which featured the water cure — lots of drinking water, baths, and fresh air. The regimen did her no good.

One day a former patient of Vail's visited the institute, healed of his ailments and extolling the virtues of Quimby. Patterson felt that Quimby's treatment was her last hope and renewed her efforts to visit him. Peel reported that at last the family arranged for Patterson, accompanied by her brother Samuel and his wife, to travel to Maine. The short trip to Portland was the beginning of a much longer odyssey for Mary Baker Patterson.

Mrs. Mary M. Patterson, of Swampscott, fell upon the ice near the corner of Market and Oxford streets, on Thursday evening, and was severely injured. She was taken up in an insensible condition and carried to the residence of S. M. Bubier, Esq., near by, where she was kindly cared for during the night. Dr. Cushing, who was called, found her injuries to be internal, and of a very serious nature, inducing spasms and intense suffering. She was removed to her home in Swampscott yesterday afternoon, though in a very critical condition.

This short article in the Saturday, February 3, 1866 issue of *The Lynn Reporter* described Mrs. Eddy's (then Mrs. Patterson) fall on the ice. It was this experience that was pivotal to her development of Christian Science.

— 4 —

Beginnings

WHEN PATTERSON AR-
RIVED AT THE INTER-
national Hotel in Portland, she had to be carried up the
stairs to her room. After resting for a while, she made her
way to the waiting room, where she finally met Phineas
Parkhurst Quimby.

Quimby, born in 1802, worked in his younger years as a
clock maker and inventor. As Peel reported, Quimby was an
inquisitive man, and a lecture he attended in 1838 changed
his life — a lecture on hypnotism, or as it was known in
the 19th century, mesmerism. Mesmerism was named after
Franz Anton Mesmer, a Viennese doctor who treated disease by a revolutionary method. He postulated the existence
of a mysterious, unseen magnetic fluid connecting all living
organisms and believed that his treatments affected this fluid
and so cured his patients. Actually, he hypnotized them and
then suggested that they think of themselves as being well,
although it is doubtful he realized this. By the late 20th
century, hypnotism has been extensively studied and has
been used with mixed results to treat people for addictions
and pain. In the 19th century, mesmerism was a mysterious

process with overtones of spiritualism and the occult. Interest in mesmerism became a wildly popular fad that swept through the United States in the 1840s. Quimby discovered that he was a talented mesmerist and, as Peel noted, proceeded to expand his efforts from performing in traveling exhibitions to healing in a medical practice.

By the time Patterson traveled to see him, Quimby no longer considered himself a mesmerist; rather, his circular announced, "his explanation is the cure." During most treatments, he would wet his fingertips with water and touch the patient's head while explaining the illness. In other cases, he simply talked to patients. Many times, his treatments were effective; they represented what would later be thought of as an early form of psychological therapy. He attempted to analyze his mind cures and write about them — sometimes in religious terms. He basically believed that the human mind could both cause and cure disease. He also was of the opinion that the miracles recorded in the New Testament as performed by Jesus were examples of "mind cure" but ignored what Patterson later came to see as a crucial difference between the power of the human mind and the power of God.

At first, his system seemed to work in Patterson's case. A week after her arrival, she was able to walk up 182 steps to the dome of the Portland city hall. She was filled with enthusiasm for Quimby's method. In the first of many letters to the local newspapers, she proclaimed to the *Portland Evening Courier* that Quimby "heals as never man healed since Christ." Soon she was able to share her elation with her husband.

Dr. Patterson escaped from a Confederate prison in September 1862 and rejoined his wife in Portland. After the

PHINEAS PARKHURST QUIMBY

Phineas Quimby was a clock maker and inventor before he became a practitioner of mind cure. He claimed to cure patients' physical ailments by explaining their diseases to them. Patterson found his ideas very interesting and spoke of him with appreciation even after her own ideas developed in a different direction.

couple went to stay with the Tiltons in Sanbornton, Mary Patterson wrote to Quimby, "I am to all who once knew me, a living wonder, and a living monument of your power. . . ." But eventually, away from Quimby's presence, she found her condition worsening. Additionally, she struggled to reconcile Quimby's techniques and somewhat confusing theories about the healing power of the mind with her lifelong convictions as a Christian. Around that time, she remarked to an acquaintance, "If all diseases are unreal and not good, God who is good and real should be our only healer, and I believe that if we only knew how to ask Him we should need no other."

She returned to Portland in the middle of 1863. She spent entire afternoons with Quimby, observing his treatments of others and discussing his theories. Quimby called her a "devilish bright woman" and enthusiastically shared his ideas. Her fellow boarders remembered her staying up late into the night writing.

She spent most of the next year in Portland or visiting new friends in Maine. Her husband was finding it difficult to settle back into practice after his experiences in the Civil War, but eventually the Pattersons wound up in Lynn, Massachusetts, and then in a nearby community called Swampscott. All was not well between them, for Dr. Patterson had little patience with his wife's new enthusiasm and even less with her continuing struggle to explain Quimby's healing work in Christian terms. On the other hand, his wife found rumors of his flirtations with women patients especially distressing. Nevertheless, she settled down and made a number of friends in Lynn, particularly after she joined the Linwood Lodge, a branch of the Good Templars, a social organization dedicated to promoting temperance (moderation or abstinence regarding alcohol), a very popular cause at the time.

Mrs. Patterson's troubles continued, however. Her father, Mark Baker, died in October 1865 and left all his money to his son George, the only one of his sons to produce an heir. Dr. Patterson began traveling again, which upset his wife, and when he was home, as Peel discovered through checking newspapers of the period, he embarrassed himself by engaging in a public dispute with another dentist on the subject of patient billing. She suffered another blow in January 1866, when Phineas Quimby died, a victim of cancer. More alone than ever, her health came to a crisis several weeks later in a way that changed her life.

On Thursday, February 1, 1866, Patterson was walking with friends to a meeting of the Good Templars. The ice-packed sidewalk proved treacherous, and she slipped and fell violently. Knocked unconscious from the impact, she was carried to a nearby house and diagnosed as having a concussion and possible spinal dislocation. Her friends immediately called a homeopathic doctor and surgeon, Alvin Cushing. They thought that she might die, or at the very least, never walk again.

The next morning, she regained consciousness and begged to be taken home, although Cushing recommended that she not be moved. Cushing gave her an injection of morphine to lessen the pain, and she slipped into unconsciousness. Her friends wrapped her in fur robes, put her in a sleigh, and drove her home.

Peel's research into the incident revealed the ensuing events. All day Friday, concerned friends and acquaintances came to visit, and one of them sent for the minister of her church. On Saturday, the doctor visited again and felt he could do no more, although she had not improved. More well-wishers visited her on Sunday, including the Reverend Jonas Clark, who prayed for her but felt it necessary to prepare her for the worst, and a friend, Mrs. Ira Brown. As Brown left Patterson's bedside, Patterson claimed, "When you come down the next time, I will be sitting up in the next room."

"Mary, what on earth are you talking about!" Brown incredulously replied.

Later that afternoon, in private, Patterson opened her Bible to the New Testament and was healed as she read an account of Jesus' healing the sick. She got out of bed, put on her clothes, and walked into the parlor. The Reverend Jonas Clark, who had come back, thought he was seeing a ghost. Patterson had evidently recovered from her injuries, but more importantly, she had undergone a profound change as she studied the Bible that afternoon. Years later, she tried to explain: "That short experience included a glimpse of the great fact that I have since tried to make plain to others, namely, Life in and of Spirit; this Life being the sole reality of existence." In *Retrospection and Introspection* she recalled: "Even to the homœopathic physician who attended me, and rejoiced in my recovery, I could not then explain the *modus* of my relief. I could only assure him that the divine Spirit had wrought the miracle." She understood her healing as resulting from a tangible awareness of God. She later told a friend that she then "noticed that when she had entertained similar thoughts in connection with the ills of her neighbors they too were benefited." The whole event was crucial to her development of Christian Science.

After Patterson recovered, her situation presented new

challenges. Her friends' skepticism about her cure troubled her deeply, and she spent much time studying the Bible and pondering the experience. More mundane affairs needed her attention also: Her husband disappeared from Lynn, leaving her unable to pay her rent — $1.50 per week — and she was evicted from her rooms. Mrs. Patterson then stayed with some friends, the Phillipses, where she healed a painful infection in their son's finger by her new understanding of prayer. Dr. Patterson returned in July and moved with his wife to Mrs. George Clark's boardinghouse. One month later he deserted her permanently. They had grown too different, and evidence that pointed to his involvement with other women may have proved the final straw.

Patterson moved from boardinghouse to boardinghouse and stayed with friends as long as they would have her. She set to work to understand more fully what had happened to her in February in Swampscott. She continued to pray and study the Bible for hours and then wrote commentaries on her readings. Possibly, as Peel pointed out, her religious struggles and single-minded determination to "find the science that governed" the healing process annoyed her hosts and contributed to her many moves. Apparently, it troubled her remaining family in New Hampshire.

Abigail and Alexander Tilton had become two of the most highly esteemed — and prosperous — citizens of Sanbornton, which would soon be renamed Tilton. Smaus reported the correspondence between the sisters and noted that Abigail was even able to offer to build a house for her sister, next to her own large residence. However, Smaus also recorded that Tilton added: "There is only one thing I ask of you, Mary, that you give up these ideas which have lately occupied you, that you attend our church and give over your theory of divine healing."

Patterson declined; she could not abandon "this one thing I do." Estranged from much of her family, separated from her husband, and far from her son, she spent the next few lonely years moving constantly. In the autumn she boarded with the Ellises of Swampscott, Massachusetts. Fred Ellis remembered her writing all day in her room until she came into the parlor, where "she would read the pages to Mother and me, inviting, almost demanding, our criticisms and suggestions."

In the Clark boardinghouse where she stayed again later that fall, Patterson joined 13 other boarders each night for dinner, where she sat at the head of the table. George Clark, then a young man, remembered she "easily dominated attention when she cared to talk, and she was always listened to with interest. Every one liked and admired her, though sometimes her statements would cause a protracted argument."

She spent hours writing an exegesis (verse-by-verse interpretation) of the Book of Genesis, in which Peel noted the development of her ideas about the nature of God, spiritual life, and Christian healing. Her ideas were interesting to many, especially to a young shoemaker named Hiram Crafts, who stayed in the Clark boardinghouse whenever he came to Lynn as temporary summer help in the shoe factories. Patterson began to teach him about healing. When the time came for Crafts to leave Lynn, he asked Patterson to return with him and his wife to his hometown of East Stoughton, Massachusetts. In return for room and board, she continued to teach and advise Crafts about her newly discovered science of healing.

Crafts gave up his cobbling trade to become a healer. The following spring, the Crafts household moved to the larger town of Taunton, and in May 1867, an advertisement appeared in a local newspaper addressed "To The Sick" and continuing, "Dr. H. S. Crafts, would say unhesitatingly, *I can cure you.*" The announcement went on to say Crafts had successfully treated consumption, dyspepsia, and rheumatism, as well as "many other forms of disease and weakness," and included a testimonial from a satisfied patient.

Good reports from his patients soon swelled his practice. During the evenings, Patterson continued to instruct and encourage him. The association, however, did not last the year. Mrs. Crafts complained bitterly about the large amount of time Patterson spent with her husband. Patterson packed her trunk and moved on.

On the recommendation of friends, she went to Amesbury, Massachusetts, where "Mother" Webster, a kind spiritualist who ran an informal boardinghouse, took her in. Although Patterson was not a spiritualist and differed greatly with her hostess's beliefs and practices, Webster gave Patterson a large, sunny room and her own desk, where Patterson continued working on her exegesis of the Book of Genesis.

Webster had always opened her home to invalids. Patterson mingled with the sick and performed several cures. Rumors crisscrossed the town that a woman living at the Websters' could perform miracles. When Patterson and Webster took their evening walk to the river, curious townspeople sometimes loitered on the bridge speculating derisively that Patterson might decide to walk on water.

Patterson, who would eventually be granted a divorce, declined to use the name of her second husband any longer and preferred to be known as Mrs. Glover. She decided to teach her healing practices again but to a larger audience. On July 4, 1868, she advertised for "any person desiring to learn how to heal the sick." She promised there was "no medicine, electricity, physiology or hygiene required," and added, "No pay required unless this skill is obtained."

Before the lessons could commence, however, Webster's son William Ellis returned to the house, as he did each year in preparation for his family's summer occupancy. When Glover and two other guests had not left because they did not have other lodgings, they were ejected into the rainy night. They located temporary lodgings down the street at the residence of Sarah Bagley, where they lived during the summer of 1868. In *Mary Baker Eddy: The Years of Discovery,* Peel traced Glover's subsequent actions.

One of the fellow guests, Richard Kennedy, was only 19 years old and worked in a small box factory, but he, Bagley, and Glover became a trio of rather unlikely friends. Glover soon began discussing her research into healing with Bagley and Kennedy, and in the evenings, Bagley, Kennedy, and Glover read the Bible and the manuscripts Glover had worked on during the day. When she had to move again because Bagley needed a boarder who could afford to pay more rent, Glover went to stay with the Wentworths, acquaintances in Stoughton. During the 19 months she spent in Stoughton, she continued to instruct Kennedy through the mail and when he managed to visit her.

At first, the Wentworths were delighted to have Glover

Sometime during the 1860s, Patterson visited a photographer's studio, where she sat for a series of pictures. While waiting to be photographed, Patterson quieted a crying child. The photographer took their picture together. Despite the difficulties of her situation during those years, wherever she stayed she always maintained a kindly interest in her hosts' children.

stay with them. Although she spent long hours in her room completing her notes and musings on the Book of Genesis, and began writing a manuscript, called at various times by different names including both *The Science of Soul* and *The Science of Man,* to be used to teach her new system of healing, she was never too tired to invite the children to her room at the end of the day for backgammon, games, and singing. As Glover worked away at her manuscript, her thoughts crystallized, and she developed a growing conviction that genuine Christian healing is based on divine law rather than personal contact or influence — an understanding that bore fruit in the consistent healing of sickness and sin, in her view. Finally, she decided that her book was ready to be published and turned all her energy to that aim. She inquired in Boston and found a publisher who was willing to print the book — for a fee of $600. The Wentworths' enthusiasm toward their guest cooled, possibly, as Peel speculated, because she asked them to help with this cost. She left their home in late March 1870 and went to stay with Bagley again. There she resolved to take a new course in life. She had begun referring to her practice of healing as Moral Science and was determined to prove that it was effective — not only to her fellow boarders, hosts, and hostesses but also to the public. Late in the spring of that year, Glover and Kennedy signed a partnership agreement that was to last three years. Glover would teach; Kennedy would heal according to her teachings.

They relocated to Lynn and sublet five rooms on the second floor of a small private school. The rooms contained little furniture; the new tenants covered the floors with oilcloth and the windows with cheap shades. Outside on a tree, they hung a sign announcing simply DR. KENNEDY.

One of the houses in which Mrs. Patterson lived in early 1866 was the Newhall House in Swampscott, Massachusetts. From 1866 to 1870 she moved constantly between boardinghouses and friends' homes while working on her writing and developing her discovery of Christian Science, which she referred to as Moral Science at the time.

To set oneself up as a doctor and espouse a wholly new system or science of healing might seem ludicrous in the 20th century, but in the small towns of America in the 1800s it was not unusual. Neither medical practice nor medicines were regulated, and the popular press was filled with the announcements of esoteric cures, dubious physicians, and practitioners of electrical treatment, magnetic treatment, and phrenology (a method of evaluating character and aptitude by careful observation of the natural bumps on a person's skull). In the beginning, Kennedy and Glover were two among many, but they soon became quite successful.

On July 15, Glover noted to Bagley, "I have all calling on me for instruction . . . Richard is literally overrun with patients." She advertised again to teach classes in Moral Science. The first class consisted of 12 lectures over the course of 3 weeks. The 5 or 6 students agreed to pay $100 each and a percentage of earnings from their future practice.

Each student read and memorized in part a handwritten copy of *The Science of Man,* which she had copyrighted in 1869 but did not publish, in a much revised version, until 1876. Later, she said that her early "compositions were crude, — the first steps of a child." One student in a later class commented that reading her manuscripts was, "compared to her expounding of them, as the printed page of a musical score compared to its interpretation by a master." Even students who later abandoned her science told others of the "emotional exultation" Glover imparted in her classroom.

After the final lesson, Glover wrote each student a congratulatory letter, addressing them by their new title of doctor. For the next series of classes, she raised her fee to

$300, one-third of the average shoe worker's yearly salary. Yet students still flocked to her.

Reports exist of how Glover instantaneously healed people of several types of diseases. A number of her students also practiced successfully, but sometimes they, like Quimby, laid their hands on their patient's head during treatment — a practice with which Glover felt increasingly uncomfortable. She later wrote in *Miscellaneous Writings,* "Although *I* could heal mentally, without a sign save the immediate recovery of the sick, my students' patients, and people generally, called for a sign — a material evidence wherewith to satisfy the sick that something was being done for them. . . . "

Peel records in *The Years of Discovery* one particularly disruptive result of the controversy over her students' physical manipulation of patients. A disgruntled member of her third class, Wallace Wright, charged her with teaching mesmerism. As reported by Peel, in early 1872, Wright published his allegations in the *Lynn Transcript* in an article called "Moral Science, alias Mesmerism"; Glover replied in the same newspaper; Wright attacked again and the two engaged in a fierce public debate. Part of one of Glover's replies indicates the direction her Moral Science — which was the name she first used for her system of healing — would take. Glover began by explaining that "Moral Science belongs to God, and is the expression or revelation of love, wisdom, and truth. . . . All that He [God] hath made is harmonious, joy-giving and eternal. . . . Moral Science is to put down sin and suffering through the understanding that God created them not, nor made he man to be the servant to his body." She concluded by noting that she knew nothing more of the practice of mesmerism "than does a

A crowd of young people stand outside the building where Glover and a student taught and practiced Moral Science in the spring of 1870. The first floor housed a private girls' school; Glover held her highly successful — and unique — classes in Moral Science on the floor above.

kitten . . . Whereas I do claim to understand the Moral and Physical Science that I teach." Wright then publicly challenged her to, among other things, "walk on the water." When Glover ignored this sarcastic request, Wright noted her silence and wrote, "Mrs. Glover and her science are virtually dead and buried."

Both Glover and her science were doing quite well, but Wright's attack made her ponder whether or not elements of Quimby's practices persisted in her teachings. She saw Christian healing through prayer as sharply diverging from hypnotic suggestion, and to make the point clear she instructed her students to erase from their manuscripts a brief reference to physical manipulation. Many rebelled. In particular she insisted that Kennedy stop rubbing his patients' heads while treating them, as he often did. Kennedy refused. The disagreement was acrimonious and Kennedy destroyed their contract. Although Glover continued to work with him for three months, she was unable to resolve the situation and on May 11 their partnership was dissolved. A few days later she left Massachusetts for a series of visits to her family in New Hampshire.

Nothing remained to her there: Her brothers George and Samuel had died in 1867 and 1869, respectively. She was estranged from her sister, Abigail; her sister Martha had gone west to Kansas with her daughter and son-in-law. Glover moved on to visit her widowed stepmother, eventually returning to Lynn.

In later years, she recalled that while engaging in the battle of letters with Wright in the *Lynn Transcript,* she had turned to her Bible, opened it, and read verse 8 in chapter 30 of the Book of Isaiah: "Now go, write it before them in a table, and note it in a book, that it may be for the time

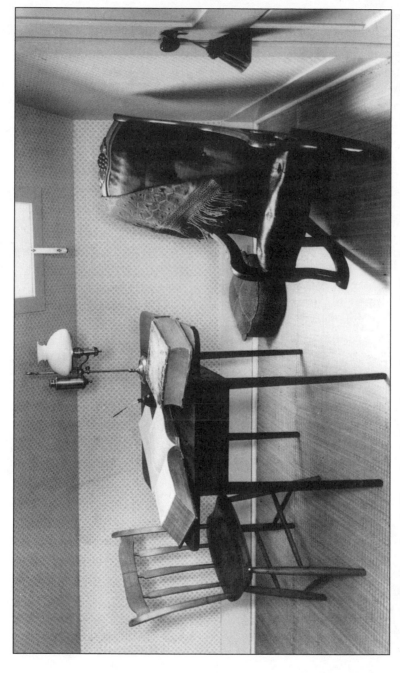

A photograph of Glover's skylit attic workroom at 8 Broad Street in Lynn reveals its sparse furnishings. Glover labored there over the final pages of the first edition of *Science and Health.*

to come for ever and ever." She promptly suspended all her classes to free herself to write a book. Once again she moved from house to house, concentrating all her efforts on her writing.

In late 1873 the book, then titled *The Science of Life,* was rejected by a publisher. She went back to work on it; it was rejected again in early 1874, according to Peel. Some of her students urged her not to waste her time on a book few would ever comprehend. But after more rewriting and rejections, two students agreed to pay a Boston printer named W. F. Brown to bring the book out, and the manuscript was sent to the printer on September 5, 1874.

In March 1875, she noticed that a house at 8 Broad Street was for sale. She saw it as the answer to her prayers, the chance to escape her housemates' wagging tongues and critical glances. She managed to buy the house and financed expenses by renting out most of the first floor to tenants. On the third floor, in a tiny skylighted bedroom, she struggled with proofreading the printer's text of her book and adding 14 pages in which she firmly disavowed mesmerism. Few but herself entered the room. Downstairs, in the small parlor she reserved for her use, she taught another class of four students.

While putting the finishing touches on her manuscript, she tried to find the perfect title for it. One night, as she stared through the skylight at the stars, the title came to her. She rose from her bed immediately and wrote down *Science and Health.* From her youngest days her ambition had been to write a book, but *Science and Health* was in some ways more than just a book. It was to become the foundation of a worldwide religion.

Eddy, serene and confident, sat for this portrait holding a book in the early 1880s. During this time, and in later periods, as Eddy struggled with both the organizational and spiritual questions that the establishment of the Christian Science church entailed, she regularly turned to the Bible for guidance.

— 5 —

Beyond Lynn

WHILE GLOVER AWAIT-
ED THE PUBLICATION
of *Science and Health,* Christian Science (as she and her
students had begun calling their healing method and philosophy) began slowly changing and taking on form. In
June 1875, as Peel reported, eight of her students banded
together and ". . . arranged with the said Mary Baker
Glover, to preach to us or direct our meetings on the Sabbath of each week . . . ." They also resolved to contribute a
small amount of money every week that "shall be expended
for no other purpose or purposes than the maintenance of
said Mary Baker Glover as teacher or instructor, [and] than
the renting of a suitable hall." Among the students who
signed the resolution were Daniel H. Spofford, whose wife
had taken a class with Glover five years earlier, and George
Barry. Both were particularly devoted to Glover and the
cause of Christian Science.

Always a devout Congregationalist, Glover had expected
that her healing ministry would be accepted by the established Christian churches. Her early students testified about
their experiences in Christian healing at their individual

churches, only to hear several ministers denounce such testimony as "blasphemous." It became apparent that the revolutionary theological ideas in *Science and Health* might only be welcome in a revolutionary new religion.

Several of her early students, as Peel noted, reported that Glover had exclaimed to them, "Some day I shall have a church of my own!" She took a step further, her biographer observed, from her old church when she formally resigned on June 13, 1875, from the Congregational church in Tilton, which she had joined 37 years earlier. For five weeks following her students' resolution she did lead Sabbath meetings at the Good Templars' hall in Lynn, but then she stopped, busy with the details of having her book published. The time to found a true church had not yet come.

The printer completed 1,000 copies of *Science and Health* on October 30, 1875. Published reviews appeared occasionally. Critics wrote, "This book is indeed wholly original, but it will never be read." The idea that a woman would attempt to create theological principles merely amused other critics, one of whom suggested that Glover "devote her remaining years to healing the sick, and leave the writing of books upon philosophy and religion to others."

Glover sent spirited responses to her critics, especially to clergymen who ridiculed her. Other readers were more favorably impressed. Peel noted that among them was Bronson Alcott, a respected New England philosopher and the father of Louisa May Alcott, who wrote *Little Women*. Alcott visited Glover and her students in Lynn and commended their work. Meanwhile, as curious readers passed the book among themselves, increasing numbers believed *Science and Health* to be the most important book they had ever read. Some readers were healed of illnesses. Others resolved to travel to Lynn to be healed by Glover. A sign announcing Mary B. Glover's Christian Scientists' Home welcomed each arrival.

Glover explained that she named her science "Christian" because "it is compassionate, helpful, and spiritual," and has as its basis the life and teaching of Jesus. She wrote in *Science and Health,* "Christian Science is the law of Truth, which heals the sick on the basis of the one Mind or God. It can heal in no other way, since the human, mortal mind so-called is not a healer, but causes the belief in disease."

Basically, she held that God is wholly good and all-powerful, the Principle or source of all that is real. To express more of God's infinite nature she also referred to God variously as Father-Mother, Love, Mind, Soul, Spirit, Truth, and Life (which she capitalized in this context). She held that if God is all and is only good, then all that is not good — including sin, disease, and death — is a denial of God and not ultimately real, however challenging it seems in our human experience. She saw matter itself as a misconception of reality, and healing as pointing to the deeper spiritual reality of life in and of God. Prayer, in her view, involved not asking God for miracles but gaining a fuller sense of this ever-present Love and Life. She regarded the accounts of Jesus' healing in the New Testament as examples of Christian practice today.

Glover maintained that Christian Science, like other sciences, could be consistently proven through demonstration, as Jesus Christ had done. "He proved what he taught," she wrote. "This is the Science of Christianity. Jesus *proved* the Principle, which heals the sick and casts out error, to be divine. Few, however, except his students understood in the least his teachings and their glorious proofs, — namely, that

A sign identifies the house at 8 (now 12) Broad Street in Lynn as Mary B. Glover's Christian Scientists' Home. Asa Gilbert Eddy is visible sitting in the right-hand window directly beneath the sign. The first practitioner to identify himself as a Christian Scientist, Asa married Mary on New Year's Day in 1877.

Life, Truth, and Love (the Principle of this unacknowledged Science) destroy all error, evil, disease, and death."

In the home at 8 Broad Street, several students lived with Glover, engaged in the learning and practice of Christian Science. She resumed teaching and began organizing her small but growing following, which included several newcomers to Lynn, among them Asa Gilbert Eddy. In July 1876, Glover formed the Christian Scientist Association to bring students together for continuing education and Christian fellowship and to nurture the understanding and practice of spiritual healing.

Six months later, on January 1, 1877, she married Asa Gilbert Eddy, whom she affectionately called Gilbert. Eddy, a former sewing machine salesman, was the first practitioner to identify himself as a Christian Scientist on his office sign, as several biographers have noted. A soft-spoken, gentle man, he readily accepted his position as his wife's helpmate. "Mrs. Eddy is the rightful head [of the movement]," he said, "and we have never yet succeeded unless she filled that place."

The wedding was performed by a Unitarian minister, and four weeks later the Eddys' friends threw a party for them, complete with gifts, wedding cake, and lemonade. The change in circumstances, however, precipitated a series of power struggles, especially among some of the male Christian Scientists. Daniel Spofford and George Barry, as Peel pointed out, were particularly upset by the marriage of their leader. Some historians, noting that Spofford had unsuccessfully sued for divorce in November 1876, believe that he wished to marry Glover himself and his disappointment and frustration may explain the force of his later actions toward the Eddys, which Peel extensively detailed, along with those of Barry. Peel's explanations greatly clarify the events of this troubled period.

Three months after Eddy's marriage, Barry sued her for $2,700, claiming that he had performed duties at 8 Broad Street for which he deserved to be paid. The bitterness of her former student troubled Eddy greatly, and the suit was not settled until 1879.

Daniel Spofford, recently appointed Eddy's publisher, wrote her on May 30 regarding a second edition of *Science and Health*. His distress about other matters filled the missive, in which he claimed, . . ."the 'writing on the wall' is . . . 'you have proven yourself unworthy to be the standard bearer of Christian Science,' and God will remove from you the means for carrying on this work." He concluded, "I propose to carry it [the cause] alone."

Spofford was expelled from the Christian Science Association in December 1877. His rancor toward Eddy grew and embroiled both her and Christian Science in two bizarre and well-publicized lawsuits during the next year. His behavior also prompted her to define more clearly what she came to see as the hypnotic influence of hatred on human thought and to warn her students of its negative effects. Peel explained her view by noting, "The unwary recipient [of malicious suggestions] could be led to accept induced states of mind as the product of his own thinking, just as the skillful advertiser can make impressionable consumers believe that they passionately desire products of little use or value to them." In several of Eddy's letters at the time and in the revision of *Science and Health* she was working on, she explains that such projected hatred is the opposite of prayer.

She used the term *animal magnetism* — the 19th-century term for hypnotism — to describe this phenomenon.

Around this time, the bank in which Gilbert Eddy had invested their savings failed, while Barry's lawsuit was still going on and threatened to prove costly. Edward J. Arens, another student, was eager to help. He suggested that the Eddys sue renegade students.

First, Arens helped file a suit against Richard Kennedy for unpaid tuition to Mrs. Eddy and shortly afterward against several other early students for the same reason. Kennedy lost the suit but appealed the verdict and asked for a trial by jury. Arens seems to have been enamored of legal proceedings, for the suits he promoted did not end there. Battles between former students and Eddy soon spilled into several courtrooms and across the tabloids.

However, the so-called Salem Witchcraft Trial of 1878 overshadowed all the other proceedings. Miss Lucretia Brown, a student of Christian Science and former patient of Spofford's, accused him of maliciously using his mind to injure her health. Brown's request for a trial shows how very upset she was, and Peel observed that her fears of Spofford's malice certainly could have made her sick.

The proceedings were marked by great publicity, most of it adverse to Eddy and the Christian Scientists. The popular sensationalist newspapers of the day made the most of the unusual charge and the unusual woman at the center of it. Mrs. Eddy conducted herself calmly, and the trial never took place. The judge decided it was not in the power of the court to restrain Spofford's mind.

Her own lawsuits and those of her students brought her

to the view that such dissension could be healed only through relying more wholly on divine Love.

Eddy had need of aid, for October 1878 was filled with troubles. That month a revised edition of *Science and Health* appeared, but the printer was incompetent and the book was practically ruined. Eddy was greatly distressed, for the book represented years of work and her effort to communicate her discovery to others. A calamity of a more personal nature followed. Just a few days later, Dr. Eddy and Arens were arrested on spurious charges of conspiring to murder Spofford, who had disappeared from his home on October 15 and whose body had supposedly been identified in the morgue. At the time of the arrest, however, he turned up quite healthy. The *Boston Globe* nevertheless reported:

> Finding that they could not dispose of their rival by any process of law, the Eddy combination next resorted to stronger measures . . . [they] visited Boston and bargained with a Portland street "bummer" to put Dr. Spofford out of the way, in other words, to MURDER HIM IN COLD BLOOD.

The reporters gleefully painted the Eddys in the worst possible light. Their religion, their home — almost every aspect of their life differed greatly from the norm for a small 19th-century town, which made them fair prey for gossipmongers. During the height of the sensation, Kennedy's appeal came to trial, and the jury of Lynn residents, influenced by all the publicity, overturned the earlier verdict. Eddy's attorney appealed, but in the end the case was discontinued because important documents disappeared.

The charges against Asa Eddy were eventually proven to be a contrived attempt to damage his wife. The evidence was bizarre and convoluted, and much of the testimony

In 1861, George Glover established contact with his mother for the first time in more than five years; two years later he posed for this photograph. In 1879, he traveled to Boston to visit his mother — the first time the two had met in 23 years.

turned out to be perjuries. Although it was a very difficult period, Eddy would later write, "Every trial of our faith in God makes us stronger."

In support of Christian Science, Eddy's strength could not be doubted. Even before the charges against her husband had been dropped, Peel recorded, Eddy began journeying to Boston each week to lecture at the Baptist Tabernacle. Some Sundays the audience cheered, clapped, and stamped for Eddy as she answered the questions of her detractors, including the presiding clergyman. In January she wrote, "I have lectured in parlors 14 years. God calls me now to go before the people in a wider sense."

On April 12, 1879, the Christian Scientist Association voted to establish a church. The 26 members invited Eddy to the pastorate. On August 23, Massachusetts granted a charter to the Church of Christ, Scientist, which according to its members was "designed to commemorate the word and works of our Master [Jesus Christ], which should reinstate primitive Christianity and its lost element of healing." (These words are recorded in the *Manual of the Mother Church*.) The Christian Scientists continued to hold simple services in Boston and in various members' homes. Their services consisted of silent prayer, the Lord's Prayer, a sermon by Mrs. Eddy based on a passage from the Bible, and questions and answers.

The Eddys eventually spent the winter of 1879–80 in Boston, where the Church of Christ, Scientist, grew and flourished. Mrs. Eddy taught several classes and enjoyed a visit from her son George Glover, who, after travels through the West, settled in Deadwood in the Colorado Territory, where he married and had a child. Eddy and Glover were happy to see each other, for although they had continued corresponding, they had not met in 23 years. George spent a few months with his mother and stepfather but showed little interest in joining his mother's church.

The following summer the Eddys went to Concord, New Hampshire, where Mrs. Eddy worked on a third edition of *Science and Health*. During this period she thought much about organizing and strengthening the burgeoning Christian Science movement. As the church grew, she wished to give it a solid foundation. A properly printed, up-to-date version of *Science and Health* was a necessity, because every Christian Scientist studied the volume along with the Bible. In addition, she wanted to make sure that Christian healing would remain a recognized and legitimate method of treatment. Peel noted that in February 1880, a bill had been considered by the Massachusetts legislature that would regulate medical practice. Well meant but poorly phrased, the bill would have severely restricted any form of treatment not sanctioned by state-accredited medical schools — including the treatments of homeopaths and Christian Scientists. The bill had been defeated, but it made Eddy think about how to protect her movement both from misunderstandings from within and restrictions from without. She expressed interest in forming an accredited institution to teach Christian Science healing methods. That summer, she questioned several medical doctors who thought favorably of Christian Science healing about the possibility of establishing such a college. When she returned from New Hampshire that fall, she, two doctors, and several of her students formed a corporation to run a school they named the Massachusetts Metaphysical College.

The college was not chartered until January 31, 1881, and did not begin operation until the summer of 1881. Various problems connected with publishing occupied Eddy in the interim. One problem arose from the activities of Arens, who had steadily drifted away from Christian Science after involving its founder in so much litigation in 1878. He set up his own healing practice and taught his students from plagiarized versions of Mrs. Eddy's writings. His high regard for the legal system did not include a high regard for copyright law, as Peel observed, and although the Eddys decided not to sue him, Gilbert Eddy did include a condemnation of Arens's plagiarism in a preface to the third edition of *Science and Health*. (The passage was eliminated in subsequent editions.)

In search of a trustworthy publisher for the third edition, in January 1881, Eddy called on John Wilson of the University Press in Cambridge, Massachusetts. Wilson was widely considered to be among the three outstanding book manufacturers in the United States. She told him that she could not furnish the initial payment the University Press required to publish a book, although she was certain a well-made edition of *Science and Health* would be profitable.

"There wasn't a moment's hesitation in my acceptance of that order," Wilson later recalled, as was recorded in *Mary Baker Eddy and Her Books*. "I *knew* that the bill would be paid, and I found myself actually eager to undertake the manufacture."

Wilson asked when the manuscript could be delivered to him. Eddy pulled it out of her handbag. Much surprised, Wilson asked, "You brought this on the chance of my accepting it?"

Eddy smiled. "No, not on a chance. I never doubted."

The book was published on August 17, 1881. Eddy's pleasure at finally seeing her book adequately printed and bound was brief. Two months later, eight church members in Lynn issued an astounding statement at a Christian Scientist Association meeting that read in part: "... while we acknowledge and appreciate the understanding of Truth imparted to us by our teacher ... [because of her] frequent ebullitions of temper, love of money, and the appearance of hypocrisy, [we] cannot longer submit to such leadership. ...."

The eight signatories did not appear in person when the letter was read. Eddy was deeply shocked, and so were her other students, who called the eight defectors to appear at a meeting "to answer for your unjust proceedings." These 20 or so loyal followers ordained Eddy as pastor of the Church of Christ, Scientist, the next month and, according to Peel, passed a resolution which in part stated: "Resolved, That the charges made to her [Eddy] in a letter ... are utterly false, and the cowardice of the signers in refusing to meet her and sustain or explain said charges, be treated with the righteous indignation it justly deserves."

Shortly after this, Eddy left Lynn, the site of nearly 10 years of work, with the hope of settling in a community more receptive to new ideas. She carried her cause to Boston, the nation's cultural and intellectual center, but as her letters and the recollections of friends reveal, first she and her husband took a trip in January 1882 to Washington, D.C., where Gilbert investigated copyright law to protect his wife's increasing number of publications. Mrs. Eddy visited relatives and friends, but more important, she gave a number of well-attended lectures on Christian Science. She wrote to a friend, "I have worked harder here than ever, 14 consecutive evenings I have lectured three hours." Peel recorded that her success at teaching and lecturing extended to Philadelphia, where she and her husband visited next.

By May 1882, Eddy had established the Massachusetts Metaphysical College in a rented four-story gray stone house. The college was the only school of metaphysics ever given a state charter to grant degrees. Eddy was essentially the entire teaching faculty, serving as professor of obstetrics, metaphysics, and Christian Science. Her husband was to teach along with her, but he fell ill. Mrs. Eddy frequently helped her husband when he had an attack, but her husband, knowing the many duties she was forsaking, assured her that he could handle the situation.

When he passed away in June, she was overcome with grief. She went to Vermont, where she spent a month secluded in the country with only two companions. During that time she wrote to a student, "I am situated as pleasantly as I can be in the absence of the one *true heart* that has been so much to me. . . . I never shall master this point of missing him all the time . . . but I can try, and am trying as I must — to sever all the chords that bind me to person or things material."

After four and one-half weeks in the country, Eddy returned to Boston and set to work with renewed purpose. Although she was now 61 years old and had been widowed twice, she kept up a schedule that would have exhausted a much younger person. She reopened the college and taught what were referred to as Primary Classes for two to three hours a day. C. Lulu Blackman recorded her Primary Class experience in *We Knew Mary Baker Eddy*. The first day, Eddy walked in and faced her students "as one who knew herself to be a teacher by divine right. She was every inch the teacher." Eddy's eyes silently took in each student, one by one, as if she "knocked at the door" of each student's thought, Blackman recalled.

In the second-floor classroom, Eddy sat on a small raised platform. As she kept up a constant dialogue with her students, she allowed no one to take notes, perhaps sensing that to write down her words without comprehending the spirit behind them would be of little value.

After the two-week course, the graduates could receive the degree of C.S.B., Bachelor of Christian Science. As practitioners they were prepared to receive patients, note their human needs, and pray for healing.

Eddy believed a teacher should not "dismiss students at the close of a class term, feeling that you have no more to do for them." Her mail from students — who came to Boston and then returned home to all parts of the country — arrived in bulk, and she answered in kind. Students appealed for help with difficult cases, for forgiveness for past mistakes, for the settlement of disputes.

Eddy summoned Calvin Frye, a promising former student and Christian Science practitioner, to help her with the work load. He first attended a class in 1881 and stood by her and her husband when many Lynn students defected that year, as Peel pointed out. Frye served as a secretary, spokesman, and confidant. He never left Eddy for even a single day for the next 28 years. Certainly she needed his help with daily affairs. Her many duties, she wrote, "make me too perplexed too mindworn often to think — so I would give up writing and at a late hour would crawl into bed to toss all night and half asleep give directions on business *cares* that concern the good cause."

She soon added to these cares with the founding of the *Journal of Christian Science* in 1883. As Peel reported, Eddy

Calvin Frye began to study with Eddy in Lynn in 1881. On
August 6, 1882, he joined her household and spent every day of
the next 28 years there as her secretary. His selfless devotion was
a great help to Eddy and to Christian Science.

served as the editor and chief contributor for the bimonthly publication, which she subtitled "An Independent Family Paper, to Promote Health and Morals." In her first editorial, Eddy wrote: "An organ from the Christian Scientists has become a necessity. Many questions come to the College and to the practising students, yet but little time has been devoted to their answer."

In this vein, the newspaper included a column entitled "Answers to Questions." Among the explanations of science and testimonies of healings, Eddy sprinkled jokes, poems, and stories. Its back pages were filled with announcements of Christian Scientist lectures, meetings, and services, as well as listings of Christian Science practitioners. By 1885, the publication, renamed *The Christian Science Journal,* had become a monthly magazine. It is still being published more than 100 years later.

The newspaper circulated west and abroad, increasing the influx of students from other states and countries. Eddy, now 64 years old, ceased taking individual cases in order to devote her full attention to teaching and guiding the growing religious movement. Her guidance was necessary, as an observer recalled, for it seemed to her that ". . . Mrs. Eddy's pupils had a way of floating off in a sort of ecstatic rapture and that Mrs. Eddy had her hands full keeping them down to earth."

Her more down-to-earth students had great success as speakers and healers, particularly in Chicago and New Hampshire. However, some practitioners in Chicago seemed to be straying from the course Eddy established in the Massachusetts Metaphysical College — especially those who saw her emphasis on Christian regeneration as restrictive. As she worked on corrections to *Science and Health,* which appeared in its sixth printing in September 1883, she added a glossary of biblical terms which she called "Key to the Scriptures." In addition, she pondered how to strengthen the movement in spots distant from Boston.

The following spring she went to Chicago to teach a class there and also spoke to an audience of hundreds of interested listeners, as Peel reported. When she returned to Boston, she established a Normal class in August for advanced students to equip them to teach. (The name "Normal" came from normal schools, where elementary-school teachers were trained.) Eddy dispatched the Normal class graduates and encouraged them to establish institutes and associations of their own students.

Meanwhile, Boston's socialites and literati crowded her lectures. In fashionable drawing rooms, the question of the day was, "Have you met Mrs. Eddy, have you heard her lecture, have you been to her college?" Attendance at her Sunday services at Hawthorne Hall steadily increased. People crammed the aisles, and others were turned away by signs announcing No More Standing Room. Not all the listeners were supportive, however. Clergy from many of the established churches, threatened by the popularity of her radical interpretation of the Gospel, denounced her. Peel recorded that a Methodist professor at Boston University even called her "the pantheistic and prayerless Mrs. Eddy."

Initially stung by these attacks, she soon realized they presented an opportunity to explain Christian Science to even larger audiences. In March 1885, she wrote and published a pamphlet called *Defence of Christian Science*. Within days, she was invited to appear in the pulpit of Tremont Temple, where she firmly and concisely answered questions from her detractors. The influential professors and ministers of Boston debated furiously over Christian Science, and Peel reported that during the height of the furor the *Times* of London noted that in Boston, "Scores of the most valued church members are joining the Christian Scientist branch ... and it has thus far been impossible to check the defection."

The movement's rapid extraordinary growth and success exacted a price on its founder. Nearly every hour of Eddy's day was spent in service to Christian Science. She used the quiet of the late-night hours to study and write. In the mornings, she often astounded Frye with the large volume of dictation she had spent the night composing. In the early hours before class, she corrected the mistakes of typists, printers, and proofreaders, for her list of publications had grown to include much more than *Science and Health.*

In 1885 she hired Reverend James Henry Wiggin as her literary adviser. Wiggin was to improve her manuscripts' punctuation, capitalization, and sentence construction. Eddy wrote him, "Never *change* my meaning, only *bring it out.*" Wiggin recalled, "Hundreds of dollars were sunk in a bottomless sea of corrections; yet not till the authoress was satisfied that her duty was wholly done, would she allow printer and binder to send forth her book to the world."

Rumors circulated that Wiggin, not Eddy, wrote the newest edition of *Science and Health.* A colleague of Wiggin's recalled "the glee with which Mr. Wiggin would refer to the suspicion that he was the author," and remembered Wiggin once commented, "Wouldn't it have been fine if I had ...?"

Others maintained that Eddy was no more than a plagiarist. Mental science "was not made from the Bible," one lecturer stated, but rather from Phineas Quimby's experiments in mesmerism. Eddy vigorously refuted this charge, which persisted for years, partly because one of Quimby's unpublished writings had a title similar to one of her works, as Peel observed.

On the other hand, hundreds plagiarized and misrepresented Eddy's own teachings. "There are 20 false lecturers and teachers to one that is true," Eddy wrote. Healers battled for territorial rights all across the United States. Some claimed they were Christian Scientists but Eddy was not their leader; others claimed Eddy as their own inspiration but did not follow her teaching or adhere to its rigorous demands for Christian discipleship. Meanwhile, medical doctors pressed for legislation to restrict the treatment of patients to their profession.

In 1886, Eddy formed the National Christian Scientist Association, as she wrote, in part, to shelter the "perfections" of Christian Science "from the contaminating influences of those who have a small portion of its letter and less of its spirit." Two years later, she decided to attend its annual meeting to deal with many of the movement's issues in one setting. Distressed at the personal and organizational issues that threatened the movement, she called in the *Journal* for all Christian Scientists to attend the June 1888 meeting in Chicago "for Christ's and for humanity's sake."

The Chicago newspapers hailed the arrival of the "Boston Prophetess," a term with which Eddy would have been highly uncomfortable. Despite the warm welcome, she did not plan to make any public speeches. On the convention's second day, however, 4,000 curious listeners jammed the Central Music Hall, where 800 delegates were meeting. As the pastor of the Chicago church walked her to a seat onstage, he informed her she was the advertised speaker of the day.

Eddy shook her head to indicate she had no wish to speak; the reverend persisted. She paused at the steps of the rostrum and lifted her eyes as if for inspiration. The audience rose to its feet as she mounted the stage and extemporaneously gave what many students pronounced "one of the greatest statements of Christian Science ever made from a rostrum."

The audience surged forward upon the speech's conclusion. One newspaper reported that members of the crowd "vaulted to the rostrum like acrobats," attempting to touch Eddy's hand or dress. Men and women wept together. Others recited their tales of healing.

Eddy silently acknowledged the crowd as her escorts fought a path to the door. At her accommodations, she was greeted by a hastily prepared reception from the city's wealthy residents. Pandemonium broke loose again as they pressed upon her. "Silks and laces were torn, flowers crushed, and jewels lost," one biographer reported.

Eddy withdrew to her private room. She quietly commented, "Christian Science is not forwarded by these methods." The time to change course had come again.

Guided by her deep faith and continual study of the Bible, Eddy never ceased to work toward strengthening Christian Science, in spite of her advancing age. In 1889, she dissolved the church, dissatisfied with its original structure; three years later she had reorganized the church and its institutional structure into the form it has retained throughout the 20th century.

— 6 —

The General-in-Chief

*I*N FEBRUARY 15, 1889,
EDDY APPEARED ONSTAGE
in a hall in New York City and spoke again to a huge
audience. Newspapers vied with one another to provide
their readers with colorful descriptions of this petite, well-
dressed, 68-year-old woman and her sensational triumph at
public speaking. On her return to Boston she taught the
largest class ever at the Massachusetts Metaphysical College.
She seemed to be at the pinnacle of worldly success.

By mid-1889 more than 300 applications for enrollment
at the college lay piled on Eddy's desk. Prospective students
wrote from all over North America, and the college was at
the "height of prosperity," as one prominent Scientist noted.
Yet the September *Journal* included a shocking announcement from Eddy. She wrote, "Deeply regretting the
disappointment this must occasion, and with grateful
acknowledgments to the public, I now close my college."

The decision astounded her students. Their dissent
prompted an attempt to keep the college open by hiring a
professor to succeed her. But in October she implemented

her original plan at what she felt was God's direction and closed the College.

Portents of change had been accumulating throughout the previous months, as Peel observed in *Mary Baker Eddy: The Years of Trial*. That May, Eddy had resigned as pastor of the Boston church and gone to Vermont. One month later she handed control of *The Christian Science Journal* over to the national association and settled in Concord, New Hampshire. At her suggestion, in September the Christian Scientist Association in Boston was dissolved. By the end of the year, the church as she initially established it was formally disorganized. She urged Christian Scientists to continue to do the work of healing individually and with their local churches and associations.

Peel reported that amid this whirlwind of events Eddy had written, somewhat lightly, in the July *Journal,* "For what purpose has Mrs. Eddy relinquished certain lines of labor in the field of Christian Science...? Is she writing her history? or completing her works on the Scriptures? She is doing neither, but is taking a vacation, her first in twenty-five years."

The statement gives a surprisingly human glimpse of Eddy, and other events of the period make clear she was far from being a driven monomaniac consumed with expanding the success of her movement. Some Scientists had begun to call her "Mother" as a term of endearment and loyalty. She welcomed their affection but seems to have yearned for a son who shared the deep faith that motivated her life, a desire which had been made even more pointed by an extended visit from George Glover and his family. In November 1887, the Glovers had arrived in Boston for a six-month stay. Although Eddy was very busy and tried to dissuade them from visiting, she was glad to see George, his wife, Nellie, and especially their four children. The hearty, unsophisticated Glovers were not comfortable in Boston, however, and the mother and son discovered they had less and less in common as the years went on. To Eddy's dismay she discovered that most of the family was nearly illiterate. She encouraged her son to attend to the education of his children and continued to send the family money after they went back to the West.

Around the time George arrived, a homeopathic doctor named Ebenezer J. Foster joined one of her classes at the metaphysical college. He was about the same age as George but presented quite a contrast in personality. He proved particularly helpful and devoted to her initially, and in November 1888, she legally adopted him as her son, and he took the name Foster Eddy.

The actions that Eddy took in 1889 to dismantle her organizations were impelled by more than the desire for a rest and for a family. At the time there were 250 trained practitioners, 20 churches, 90 societies, and 33 academies of Christian Science. The growth of the movement had not been smooth, however, and the organization had been subject to pressures from the society around it, struggles for power within, and attacks by those who claimed to be Christian Scientists but were not. Eddy decided to devote her time to developing the movement in new directions so that it could withstand the mounting challenges. She had no intention of letting dissension wreck Christian Science. "She had previously been the Teacher," one follower later wrote, but then "she became the General-in-chief, and the Leader."

In 1890, while living in Concord, she began the 50th

revision of *Science and Health.* In the five previous years she had managed to complete the major sixteenth revision of *Science and Health* and to write and publish: *Historical Sketch of Metaphysical Healing* (1885); *Christian Science: No and Yes* (1887); *Rudiments and Rules of Divine Science* (1887); and *Unity of Good and Unreality of Evil* (1888), in addition to articles, letters, and notes in *The Christian Science Journal.* Her tremendous output of writing had accompanied a busy schedule of teaching, lecturing, and revising each printing of *Science and Health.* However, the project that she contemplated in 1890 demanded her undivided attention.

"I have learned more of Christian Science the past year than I shall ever be able to communicate," she wrote to a friend. She had revised earlier editions of *Science and Health* in piecemeal fashion as inspiration guided her; now she worked to develop a logical progression of ideas throughout the book. It was an extremely difficult task.

When her students continued to interrupt her labors, she wrote in the September 1890 *Journal:*

> I shall not be consulted verbally or through letters as to the following: Whose advertisement shall or shall not appear in the *Journal.* The matter that should be published in the *Journal.* On marriage, divorce, or family affairs of any kind. On the choice of pastors for churches. On disaffections if there should be any between students of Christian Science. On who should be admitted as members or dropped from the membership of churches. On disease, or the treatment of the sick. But I shall love all mankind and work for their welfare.

Great personal and spiritual turmoil accompanied her work on each revision of *Science and Health,* and the 1891 edition was no exception. However, Eddy realized that because she no longer taught at the college, the book would have to carry her teachings to Christian Scientists. She labored to make it applicable and understandable to a wide variety of readers, and her single-mindedness sometimes exasperated those around her.

By the end of the summer Eddy was ready to start her church afresh with the aim of avoiding the pitfalls of "material organization." Various events during 1891 impressed her with the problems inherent in governing or organizing a church based on personal popularity. Peel recorded that in one letter to a student of Augusta Stetson, a very successful Christian Science leader in New York, Eddy wrote: "Our basis in Science is IMPERSONALITY. . . . You cannot build on *personality* or you build on *sand.*" Throughout the year she searched for and prayed to find a basis of organization for Christian Science.

A more prosaic duty also occupied her and her companions — house hunting. She needed a peaceful place in the country to do her thinking and writing, and in December 1891 she bought a farmhouse on the outskirts of Concord. In June 1892 she moved into the newly enlarged house, directed the landscaping, and named the small estate Pleasant View. Eddy arose at exactly six o'clock in the morning. She read and prayed for an hour upon awakening (she did so twice more during each day). She then strolled through the house, greeting students, inspecting their housework, and sharing a lesson or two.

After her daily walk, Frye brought in to her mountains of correspondence. Because of the great volume, she dictated many of her replies. Dinner was usually served in the middle of the day, often followed by ice cream and then an afternoon carriage drive through Concord.

Immediately before moving into Pleasant View, Eddy had had discussions with members of the Boston congregation of Christian Scientists regarding some complicated legal business connected with a deed. The complex proceedings were carefully detailed by Peel in *The Years of Trial*. The deed was for a three-sided plot of land in the fashionable Back Bay section of Boston, and Eddy was determined that a Christian Science church building should be erected there. However, legal difficulties loomed menacingly. Eddy decided not to organize her church under a state charter.

Her Boston attorneys failed to find a law to accommodate her desires. She consulted a judge who also said he knew of no appropriate law for organizing a church without a charter. She asked him "upon what was human law based?"

He reflected and then said, "Upon the divine law. But," he continued, "if the Massachusetts abstracter of law can find no such statute [regarding church organizations], how can I?"

"God has somewhere provided such a law," Eddy replied, "and I know you can find it."

Three days later the judge reported success. An obscurely worded Massachusetts law provided that officers of a church could "be deemed bodies corporate" for several purposes connected with holding donations and property. Eddy quietly acquired the plot of land herself. Upon receiving payment of one dollar, she transferred ownership of the parcel to a new Christian Science Board of Directors. The deed of trust she signed on September 1 stipulated that the board build a church on the land within five years, spending "shall not be less than fifty thousand dollars" on the church edifice. If the board did not follow all of Eddy's stipulations, the deed would revert to Eddy or to her heirs. A few weeks later, on September 23, 1892, The Mother Church, The First Church of Christ, Scientist, was organized, with a group of four directors that, although not incorporated, could arrange for building construction and other matters. Initial membership in The Mother Church numbered 32 but quickly swelled, for members of branch churches could also be members of The Mother Church. The final organization of the church was evolving.

The physical evolution of The Mother Church building was proceeding at a slower rate, although 42 students immediately contributed $1,000 each to the building fund. Eddy watched over the Board of Directors' actions closely and did not hesitate to chide them when she felt it necessary. At the beginning, the board seemed stalled and mired in inactivity while the first frost of winter — which would impede construction — neared. Eddy, convinced of the divine impulsion she felt to build, wrote to them, "Why in the name of *common sense* do you not lay the foundation of our Church as GOD BIDS YOU, AT ONCE?"

Twelve days later she wrote the inert board again, telling them exactly when to break the ground and to advertise the date in the next *Journal*. She later reminded them that, "Mr. J & Mr. K [two board members] in times past by *delay* at critical times would have lost my whole plan to save my church lot had not I *driven* them to obey."

In October 1894 it looked as if six more months would be needed to complete the church. Eddy, however, insisted the church be finished before the end of the year. She ordered the board to give up some of their "gods" — extravagant decorations such as mosaic floors, silk walls, and marble and onyx trim — rather than delay the church opening. On December 29, construction workers laid the church's concrete walkways outdoors while Christian Scientists swept, mopped, and dusted inside the church auditorium. All work stopped at midnight.

"It is done!" a speaker exclaimed at a dedicatory ceremony a week later, on January 6, 1895. She read a letter addressed to Eddy: "At last you begin to see the fruition of that you have worked, toiled, prayed for. The 'prayer in stone' is accomplished."

The church auditorium held 1,500 people. Five dedicatory ceremonies were held in succession throughout the day to accommodate all of the attendees.

On December 19, Eddy had written to the Board of Directors: "The Bible and 'Science and Health with Key to the Scriptures' shall henceforth be the Pastor of the Mother Church. This will tend to spiritualize thought. Personal preaching has more or less of human views grafted into it." Since that time, the form of the Christian Science Sunday service has changed little. Two readers, typically one male and one female, read to the congregation the week's Bible lesson from these books.

In keeping with her determination not to allow church members to venerate her personally, Eddy had declined to attend the dedication. But on a Monday afternoon in April, she traveled to Boston for a private visit. Her quiet approach was necessary in order to prevent overly enthusiastic students from ringing bells in her honor and generally creating a scene. Alone, she entered the church. Walls of a soft rose hue surrounded her. The stained-glass windows were trimmed with bronze, the floors were of mosaic; the pews of birch. She later wrote in *Miscellany* that she "knelt in thanks upon the steps of its altar." After meeting with the directors, she returned, stood at the reader's platform, and recited a psalm and the words of one her favorite hymns, which ended: "Strong Deliverer! Strong Deliverer! Still Thou art my strength and shield."

She gave her first address in The Mother Church in May. While in Boston, she stayed in an apartment in the church tower meant only for her use. It had been financed by the contributions of Christian Science children, dubbed the Busy Bees, and their nickels and dimes continued to furnish the room with fresh-cut flowers. Although Eddy loved flowers, she redirected the young Christian Scientists' efforts, instructing them to devote themselves and their gifts to God, not her. The next morning, Eddy spoke before the congregation. Her address, reprinted in *Miscellaneous Writings,* included the injunction:

> Beloved children, the world has need of you, — and more as children than as men and women: it needs your innocence, unselfishness, faithful affection, uncontaminated lives. You need also to watch, and pray that you preserve these virtues unstained, and lose them not through contact with the world. What grander ambition is there than to maintain in yourselves what Jesus loved, and to know that your example, more than words, makes morals for mankind!

Eddy, who accepted the title of pastor emeritus, visited the church only once more. There would be no more preaching by her or anyone else. "The word of God, not human views, should preach to humanity," she told the Reverend Irving Tomlinson, one of her students.

Just as she had ordained the Bible and *Science and*

Health as the impersonal pastor, she published the *Manual of The Mother Church* to describe its government. A group of By-Laws adopted specifically for the Boston church, these guidelines she described as "uniquely adapted to form the budding thought and hedge it about with divine Love." The *Manual* By-Laws empower the self-perpetuating Board of Directors to oversee all of The Mother Church's activity. Their actions are governed by the *Manual.*

Under the provisions in the *Manual,* the branch churches are democratically governed. A branch church can be formed in a locale upon petition of 16 Christian Scientists, 4 of whom must already be members of The Mother Church. Before that number is obtained, they may form a society. Although the *Manual* gives general directions, the branch churches may elect their own officers and vote on their own By-Laws.

In addition to the Sunday services, each Church of Christ, Scientist, holds a Wednesday public meeting in which testimonies of healing are welcomed. No other services, such as weddings or funerals, take place in the church, nor is the building used for social functions.

Each church also maintains a Sunday School for youths up to age 20 and a Reading Room where both members and inquirers can come to pray and study the Bible or Christian Science publications. They may also buy or borrow books and periodicals, ask questions of the librarian, and use computer concordances.

The *Manual* By-Laws outlined the structure and practice of the organization. While the pastor emeritus was alive, however, she was still active in directing the church's affairs. Many of the By-Laws end with provisions such as "subject to the approval of the Pastor Emeritus," and "if she objects,

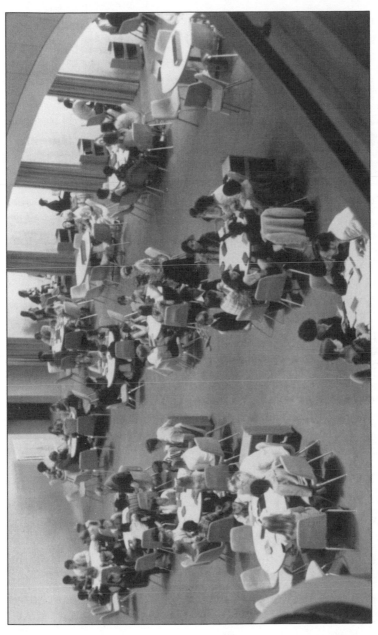

Each branch church of Christ, Scientist, maintains a Sunday School for children and teens up to age 20. Pupils learn about the healing truths of the Bible and how they can be made practical in their lives.

said candidates shall not be chosen." Within the ranks of Christian Science, she frequently hired, dismissed, and promoted officials.

One official, after an Eddy reprimand, wrote typically, "We either have a Godgiven Leader, or we have none. . . . When I enlisted in this Army I enlisted to obey orders. We are under divine orders, and you are their interpreter." On the other hand, Eddy advised her pupils to follow their leader "only so far as she follows Christ."

In February 1897, Eddy published many of her sermons, articles, letters, and poems in *Miscellaneous Writings.* In *Mary Baker Eddy: The Years of Authority,* Peel commented that the book revealed much of her personality, idiosyncratic style, and concern for the students of Christian Science. One month later, she revealed her concern even more fully. Dismayed by reports of inaccuracies in teaching, Eddy directed that all Christian Scientist instruction be suspended for one year. Because *Miscellaneous Writings* made her own words "accessible as reference," she believed, as she wrote in a letter reprinted by Peel, "Divine Science shall be taught more divinely, by the reading of Mis. Writ. The human teaching tends to liquidate the genuineness of Truth."

In addition to her continuing worries about and efforts to improve and purify the quality of instruction in the church, Eddy was worried about the behavior of Foster Eddy. Disturbing reports about him and his affairs with women impelled her to send him to Philadelphia at the end of the summer in 1896, where he could start anew. But by the summer of 1897, as Peel recorded, the Philadelphia church voted for his expulsion. Deeply saddened, Eddy finally broke with him and forbade him to visit her for at least three years.

Although Eddy barred her adopted son from Pleasant View in July, she extended an invitation to thousands of Christian Scientists to visit her that month. They had gathered in Boston at The Mother Church for the annual Communion Sunday, and her invitation to come to Concord on July 5 took them unprepared. Still, more than 2,000 journeyed north to hear her and several others speak under the hot sun.

Christian Science had grown tremendously: Regular services were even being held in London, England. One highly critical biographer, Georgine Milmine, wrote that the movement was on the threshold of becoming "the largest and most powerful organization ever founded by any woman in America." Such expansion attracted attention and curiosity — not all of it favorable. Eddy's labors on behalf of Christian Science were far from over.

A portrait painted by Alice H. Barbour shows Eddy in her later years wearing a diamond cross, a present from a devoted student. By the beginning of the 20th century, Christian Science was firmly established in the United States and had begun to attract believers from all over the world. Eddy received letters and visits from American congressmen, British nobility, and French and German Christian Scientists.

— 7 —

The Cross
and the Crown

A S THE 19TH CENTURY DREW TO A CLOSE, Eddy was approaching her 80th year. Christian Science was well established in the United States; The Mother Church welcomed throngs of loyal Scientists at every Communion Sunday. The *Manual of The Mother Church* provided firm rules to guide the operation of The Mother Church and its branches, and *Science and Health* had been reprinted several hundred times and reached hundreds of thousands of readers. Still, Eddy did not rest. The year of 1898 was one of both unprecedented expansion and further consolidation for Christian Science — under Eddy's continuing direction.

The growth of Christian Science outside the United States began to gain momentum around this time. In London, England, regular Sunday services had begun in 1896. A few years later, in March 1898, a branch church of Christian Science was organized in Hannover, in northern Germany. Because the study and practice of Christian Science depend on close reading of both the Bible and *Science and Health,* pleas for a German translation of Eddy's chief work streamed in to her. She also received requests for a French translation but was exceedingly reluctant to approve any edition in either language. The years of work she put into countless revisions and corrections of her book made her aware of the precise importance of every word and the difficulty of describing spiritual insights in human language. She feared a translation could only approximate her actual meaning. (She ultimately was to agree to foreign translations of the textbook with English appearing on facing pages.)

While Eddy was dealing with the expansion of Christian Science to the international arena, the United States itself was struggling to find its place in the realm of foreign affairs. On February 15, 1898, a U.S. battleship, the *Maine,* exploded in the harbor of Havana, Cuba, a colony of Spain. At the time, Spain was harshly repressing Cuban rebels fighting for independence. The jingoist slogan "Remember the *Maine!*" glared from headlines of sensationalist newspapers and aroused public sentiment for U.S. involvement in support of Cuba against Spain, although it was never proven that Spain had anything to do with the destruction of the *Maine.* By April, Spain and the United States were at war, and by the war's end eight months later, the United States controlled the former Spanish colonies of Cuba, Guam, Puerto Rico, and the Philippines. In the midst of the fury before hostilities broke out, Eddy wrote an article entitled "Other Ways Than By War" for the *Boston Herald,* which is reprinted in *Miscellany.*

"Killing men," she wrote, "is not consonant with the higher law whereby wrong and injustice are righted and exterminated." Eddy's comments on public affairs grew out of her conviction that Science is applicable to all the needs of man. She wrote in *Science and Health,* ". . . all men have one Mind, one God and Father, one Life, Truth, and Love. Mankind will become perfect in proportion as this fact becomes apparent, war will cease and the true brotherhood of man will be established." She had no illusions, however, about the toil and self-sacrifice involved in establishing the brotherhood of man under "one Mind, one God and Father."

Although Eddy turned her attention to world affairs, her primary focus invariably was on strengthening the cause that she felt would bring healing to the world. Peel recorded some of her actions intended to accomplish this goal. In January 1898 she formed the Christian Science Board of Lectureship, composed originally of five lecturers personally chosen by herself. They traveled the country and held lectures open to all, where they explained the teachings of the Church of Christ, Scientist, and endeavored to answer the questions of those unfamiliar with but curious about the religion. That same month she created a board of trustees to run The Christian Science Publishing Society and to supervise the publication of the monthly *Journal* and of her 11 books. Before long, the society's duties expanded to include the regular production of a new publication. The first issue of *The Christian Science Weekly* (four months later the name was changed to the *Christian Science Sentinel*) appeared in September 1898 and devoted space to national and international issues.

Although Eddy no longer served as an editor, she read the periodicals closely and remained attentive to the work of the lecturers. Annie Knott, an associate editor at the publishing society, recounted in *We Knew Mary Baker Eddy* one

Annie M. Knott became a teacher and practitioner of Christian Science after studying with Eddy at the Massachusetts Metaphysical College. She spent the rest of her life in service to Christian Science, becoming a member of the Christian Science Board of Lectureship in 1898 and an editor of Christian Science periodicals in 1903. In 1919 she became the first female member of The Christian Science Board of Directors.

example of Eddy's scrutiny and concern. She recalled the time she discussed with Eddy the obstacles she was encountering as a woman giving public lectures on Christian Science. Knott reported: "... I told her I had had very few calls up to that time," because "even personal friends ... wrote me that while they would be glad to hear me, people in general preferred to have a man lecture for them. ..." Eddy responded "... in her usual energetic manner and said it would not do to let that argument stand. ... Her words were these: 'You must rise to the altitude of true womanhood, and then the whole world will want you. ...'" Knott remembered that a short time after this conversation, "I began to have numerous calls to lecture." She "felt the inspiration of Truth" as she put it, "to prove that a woman can declare the truth and heal the sick as well as a man."

The quality of Christian Science teaching continued to be of concern to Eddy. She considered the spiritual caliber and understanding of the teacher to be of the highest importance, and the number of her former students who misrepresented her instruction caused her serious concern. Only a few weeks after the first issue of the *Weekly* rolled off the presses, Eddy formed the Christian Science Board of Education to superintend the training of new teachers of Christian Science.

Eddy announced that the Board of Education would take over the administration of formal instruction. Shortly afterward, 70 Scientists received letters or telegrams asking them to come to the Christian Science Hall in Concord at four o'clock in the afternoon on November 20. Few knew what to expect. Almost all the invitees, including several from Scotland, England, Canada, and the western territories, made it to Concord, mounted the steps, and passed through the pillared portico of the small wooden building — deeply curious about what awaited.

Eddy mounted the speaker's platform at precisely 4:00 P.M. Dressed in a black moiré silk dress, a pair of white kid gloves, and a black-and-white ermine cape, Eddy stood before the 67 students. A diamond cross given by a student adorned the neckline of her dress, and she wore a pin presented by the Daughters of the American Revolution. She searched each student's face as he or she responded to roll call. Mims and Adams observed in *We Knew Mary Baker Eddy* that the men and women gathered there were lawyers, judges, former physicians, editors, and businesspeople. Many were relatively young.

Eddy taught for six hours over the two days. She examined the students extensively, preparing them to "impart a fresh impulse" to the movement's "spiritual attainments." She sought to deepen their understanding of God and to increase their confidence in their ability to heal. Many attendees recorded their memories in *We Knew Mary Baker Eddy,* and they provide an excellent picture of the impression she made. Several recalled, as George Adams did, how "she walked quickly and gracefully to the platform." Adams added, "She was vigorous and vivid and appeared much younger than her years, but there was also great meekness and holiness in her bearing," observations seconded by other students.

The class was taught through questions and answers, and Eddy sprinkled humorous anecdotes throughout her explanations. Adams wrote of one "which she used to illustrate human philosophy."

She said there once was a man who had a fox. He made a hole in the door of his house and stuck the tail of the fox through it from the inside. Very shortly a crowd had gathered outside and he went out to ask why they were there. The reply was that they were trying to figure out how the fox was able to get through such a small hole. This, said Mrs. Eddy, was human philosophy, always trying to figure out things that never happened.

The second day, one student ended her answer with the words, "and we owe it all to her [Eddy], to this beloved one who is God's messenger today."

"You have given a very beautiful exegesis of the text," Eddy replied, "but I have one objection — I may say I have one fault to find — it was not necessary to mention me."

Another student rose immediately with tears in his eyes. "Mother, how could we forget you?" he asked.

One after another, the students stood, expressing their gratitude to her. "I cannot tell you the joy this class is to me," Eddy said in closing the session. "I am so pleased and satisfied. I feel the years roll off me!"

Following this class, the Board of Education Eddy had established took on the specific task of preparing students to be teachers. Soon thereafter she also instituted a Committee on Publication to provide accurate information about Christian Science, particularly when the popular press misrepresented the denomination and its members' beliefs.

The ensuing years were ones of unprecedented growth for Christian Science. Workers overseas clamored for more reinforcements — lecturers, practitioners, and copies of Eddy's writings. The Publishing Society kept busy issuing Eddy's many books in 2 brick buildings near The Mother Church.

On Sunday, June 23, 1903, throngs of Christian Scientists stream down the steps of Boston's Mechanics Hall, where they gathered for Sunday Communion services and annual meetings. The increasing number of congregants made it necessary to build an extension onto the church.

The Society was run by a board of trustees appointed by The Christian Science Board of Directors. All of the Society's net profits went to the church.

The local and national press sought her opinion on numerous issues and themes, although she rarely granted interviews. "My time is worth more for good than to risk its *misuse. . . .*" she wrote to her Boston representative. She did, however, contribute written replies and articles. She wrote tributes upon the deaths of President McKinley, Queen Victoria, and Pope Leo XIII. She commented on moral issues in articles such as "The Prevention and Cure of Divorce."

Congressmen sought her counsel. Foreign dignitaries called upon her. In a letter to her son, she recalled being termed "the most illustrious woman on the continent." But she continued, "I am not made the least proud by it or a particle happier for it. I am working for a higher purpose."

The tremendous success of Christian Science made some doubt its "higher purpose," and one former student of Christian Science actively encouraged criticism of its founder. Josephine Woodbury began attacking Eddy in numerous newspaper articles and encouraged others to do so. Peel reported that one of the most damaging stories was one she planted in the *Chicago Inter-Ocean,* which claimed that Scientists in that city doubted Eddy was alive. Woodbury also joined a former student of Quimby's, Julius Dresser, aided by his son Horatio Dresser, in renewing the claim that Eddy had plagiarized the tenets of Christian Science from Quimby's writings and thought. Woodbury eventually sued Eddy for libel, claiming that Eddy referred to her in insulting terms in the Communion message of 1899. Once again, the newspapers were filled with wild stories and accusations. Woodbury lost the suit two years later, but Eddy suffered greatly throughout the affair, which demanded much of her time and attention. Still, she managed to revise and rearrange *Science and Health* yet again at the end of 1901, and the 226th printing came out in January 1902.

Despite attacks in the popular press, Christian Science continued to expand. In the annual Communion message of 1902, Eddy noted that the church should "purchase more land and enlarge our church edifice so as to seat the large number who annually favor us with their presence on Communion Sunday."

Three days later, 10,000 Scientists gathered at what was the largest business meeting ever held by a church in Boston. Edward A. Kimball, a member of the church and close friend of Eddy's, announced, "Our denomination is palpably outgrowing the institutional end thereof. We need to keep pace with our own growth and progress." The gathering unanimously voted to contribute $2 million to the building project.

By 1904, Eddy's letters reveal that she regarded the continuing expansion of the Christian Science movement with serious reservations. In one, reprinted by Peel, she noted: "The true Science — divine Science — will be lost sight of again unless we arouse ourselves. . . . The building up of churches, the writing of articles and the speaking in public is the old way of building up a Cause. The way I brought this Cause into sight was through *healing;* and now these other things would come in and hide it, just as was done in the time of Jesus." A 1904 letter, quoted by Peel, that she addressed to the Board of Directors was more strongly worded. She wrote: "We want the right teaching of C. S.

or *none at all.* . . . It absolutely disgusts me to hear them [students] babble the letter and after that fail in proving what they say! It is high time that they stop talking science or . . . prove their words true." For Eddy, Christian Science had to be lived — not merely discussed — to be truly successful.

Living Christian Science at Pleasant View was not always easy. As her letters reveal, Eddy could express herself quite sharply, and her dedication to the cause was absolute. The demands on her household were intense, and several members did not last too long there. She kept Frye busy with a constant stream of letters, saw numerous officers of the church, and wrote many articles. One Scientist wrote to her, "I have never known any one who could turn out work and accomplish what you do."

Scientists and the general public alike were curious about exactly what went on at Pleasant View. Their curiosity was partly satisfied when Eddy welcomed 10,000 Scientists to hear her speak in June 1903. However, Eddy was troubled by church members who occasionally lingered along the roads of Concord, hoping for a glimpse of their leader during her daily carriage ride. In response, Peel noted, Eddy wrote a By-Law, stating that church members "shall not haunt Mrs. Eddy's drive when she goes out, continually stroll by her house, or make a summer resort near her for such a purpose."

She had to state her wishes on the matter of uninvited guests and loiterers even more strongly when the dedication of the extension of The Mother Church was held in 1906. According to her letters and notes, her strictures did not arise solely from her desire for privacy and seclusion. Instead, she felt that the emphasis on her personality rather

The interior of The Mother Church in Boston.
Construction of the domed extension began in 1902; it was dedicated on June 10, 1906.

than on God was detrimental to Christian Science. Months before the dedication, she wrote firmly to the Board of Directors in Boston, "Now is the time to *throttle the lie* that students worship me or that I claim their homage."

On June 10, 1906, half a dozen services in a row were held to accommodate the 30,000 people who came to the dedication of the new building, which included a huge dome that rose 224 feet into the air and crowned the extension to the original Mother Church. A newspaper reporter wrote admiringly, "Boston is indebted to them [Christian Scientists] for one of the finest architectural achievements in this or any other city, and other denominations might profit by their example of paying for their church before dedicating it."

At the moment of dedication, 40,011 members belonged to The Mother Church. In addition, the *Journal* advertised 682 branch churches and 267 societies spread throughout the world. The grandeur of The Mother Church, the numbers of Christian Scientists, and the figure of Eddy herself captured the nation's attention.

Eddy did not attend the dedication and continued her withdrawal from the public eye. She was unwavering in her desire to make Christian Science — not her own life — the focus of inquiry and study. In spite of her efforts, her continued withdrawal fueled speculation and public curiosity about her. By October 1906, her name blazed spectacularly from the headlines of the nation's newspapers.

The front page of the first issue of *The Christian Science Monitor* included local, national, and international news. Eddy is reported to have regarded the founding of the daily newspaper as "the greatest step forward [in her work] since I gave *Science and Health* to the world." The paper remains highly respected and widely read to this day.

— 8 —

Final Steps

*I*N OCTOBER 28, 1906,
READERS OF THE *NEW
York World* opened their Sunday paper to read an astonishing headline: MRS. MARY BAKER G. EDDY DYING: FOOTMAN AND "DUMMY" CONTROL HER. Below the headline in large type, the following paragraph appeared.

> Founder of X Science Suffering from Cancer and Nearing Her End, Is Immured at Pleasant View. While Another Woman Impersonates Her in the Streets of Concord. Mrs. Leonard, Brooklyn Healer, in False Role. Drives Out Daily in Closed Carriage with Calvin A. Frye, Secretary-Footman, Who is the Supreme Power at the Eddy Home — Founder Estimated to Have Accumulated a Fortune of $15,000,000, and to Have an Income of $1,000,000 a Year, but Members of Her Coterie Say She Has Spent It All in Charity, Though No Records of Large Gifts Can Be Found.

Intrigued by the numbers of Christian Scientists, the impressive Mother Church, and the unique nature of Christian Science teaching, newspaper writers found it hard to believe that an 85-year-old woman headed such a far-flung, successful organization. Both her age and her gender made them doubt her ability. Although Eddy had always appointed officers and teachers according to her evaluation of their spiritual fitness regardless of their gender, the majority of society regarded women as "the weaker sex," and very few women had anything to do with running organizations — secular or religious. Eddy's accomplishments were astounding.

Reporters from *McClure's* magazine and the *New York World,* owned by Joseph Pulitzer, raced to publish first stories that painted Eddy as a fraud. In *The Years of Authority,* Peel presented a clear account of the ensuing publicity and strange events. In early October, two *World* reporters traveled to Pleasant View and told Calvin Frye they believed Eddy was dead and that he controlled her wealth.

On learning of this accusation the following day, Eddy decided that it would not be difficult to prove her continuing existence. She cordially met with the reporters in the afternoon, told them she had no time for interviews because of her many duties, and ended the brief session with a handshake. The reporters lingered in Concord for two more weeks, determined to find a story. They quizzed the town residents about her health. If she was not dead, perhaps she was sick. Although most of them forthrightly replied that she certainly was alive and well, the reporters were intent on their original sensationalized story and disregarded all contrary evidence.

Representatives of the nation's wire services and all of the major New York and Boston newspapers descended on Concord after the *World* article appeared. Alfred Farlow, head of the Christian Science Committee on Publication, presented the press with numerous affidavits attesting to her physical and mental health and her ability to attend to her business affairs. Peel reported that her lawyer invited Charles Corning, the mayor of Concord, who had not yet met her, to visit her and then speak to reporters about his impression. As reprinted in *The Years of Authority,* Corning told the *Boston Herald:* "I had gone expecting to find a tottering old woman, perhaps incoherent, almost senile. Instead, when she rose to greet me, her carriage was almost erect, her walk that of a woman of forty. I have seen many old ladies, but never one with the vigorous personality of Mrs. Mary Baker G. Eddy. . . ." Still, reporters stalked the Pleasant View grounds and insisted on seeing Eddy herself. Finally, she agreed that 15 were to be allowed in the drawing room for a brief interview on October 30. Peel recorded the impressions of those who were present, who noted that Eddy paused before entering the room, her hands visibly shaking as she faced this hostile onslaught of the press, and he followed this observation with an account of the questions asked.

"Are you in perfect bodily health?" the group spokesperson, Sibyl Wilbur, asked.

"Indeed I am," Eddy replied.

"Have you any other physician than God?"

Eddy stepped forward and opened her arms wide. "No physician but God. His everlasting arms are around me, and that is enough."

"Do you take a daily drive?"

"Yes," she replied crisply and turned toward the door to do so, curtailing the interview before the final question was asked.

The *World* did not give up. At the beginning of November they published articles that resuscitated the old false charge that Wiggin had written *Science and Health.* They also sent one of the two reporters who first interviewed Eddy to South Dakota, where George Glover and his family lived in a large house Eddy had given them for Christmas seven years before.

Meanwhile, *McClure's* magazine began printing a series of articles on Eddy they had been preparing for two years, written by Georgine Milmine. *McClure's* was well known for having published the work of Ida Tarbell and Lincoln Steffens, two pioneers of muckraking journalism — investigative articles that exposed the horrible working conditions in factories and the disgusting conditions prevailing in new industries. Both writers left the magazine in May 1906. *McClure's* editors were determined to keep up their reputation as investigators of the greatest reliability in their exposé of Eddy, but as later historians have discovered, the intention to dig up scandal on their subject severely biased their judgment. Peel notes that even Milmine herself admitted that some of those who spoke with her about Eddy were not "the kind of sources we would have chosen."

The first article appeared with a frontispiece portrait over a facsimile of Eddy's signature. This was not an auspicious beginning for a series in a journal that claimed to be scrupulously accurate, as Peel observed. (The photograph pictured not Eddy but a woman named Sarah Chevaillier, as friends and acquaintances of both women were quick to point out.) The series continued for several months, filled with unfounded accusations about Eddy from alienated students. A far less widely read magazine, *Human Life,* ran a contrasting series by Sibyl Wilbur, who praised Eddy lavishly. Neither series was accurate or balanced, but both were edited and published as full-length books — Wilbur's in 1908 and Milmine's in 1909. The two biographies gave rise to two very different interpretations of Eddy's life, and later authors often based their work unquestioningly on one or the other.

Eddy was deeply upset by the *McClure's* series, but the work of the *World* reporter in South Dakota eventually presented a far greater threat to her and her life's achievement. The reporter, James Slaght, convinced George Glover that his mother was mentally incompetent and helpless. Slaght and the editors of the *World* hired William Chandler, a former senator from New Hampshire, to administer legal proceedings and impress upon Glover that his mother and her fortune were controlled by Frye and the church officers. Eddy had given the Glovers a house, but Glover did not have the income to keep it up and apparently felt that Eddy owed him more financial help. Encouraged by Chandler, Glover and his daughter visited Eddy in early January 1907. Their somewhat suspicious behavior and questions led Eddy to begin thinking about appointing trustees for her property so that she would no longer be troubled by taking care of it.

Before she could do so, on March 1, a group representing Glover and others filed a lawsuit to wrest control of Eddy's property, including her copyrights, away from her. The proceeding was called the next friends suit because it was filed on her behalf by her "next friends" — Glover, his daughter, two cousins from the Baker side of her family, and her estranged adopted son, Foster Eddy — all of whom alleged she was incompetent. The *World* headline read in part: RELATIVES SUE TO CREST MOTHER EDDY'S FORTUNE FROM CONTROL OF CLIQUE. It did not note that none of the defendants named in the suit, except for Calvin Frye,

A 1909 photograph shows Eddy looking out the window of her carriage during a ride. Two years earlier, she had maintained her custom of taking a daily drive despite the furor of publicity, bizarre speculations, and unsupported accusations that swirled about her during the next friends suit. She once serenely commented on the affair, "You cannot hurt anyone by telling the truth, and no one can hurt you by telling a lie."

had anything at all to do with administering Eddy's personal financial affairs.

The harm that the suit might do to Christian Science was uppermost in Eddy's mind, but throughout the barrage of publicity she remained confident, secure in her conviction of the power of divine law even when human law seemed to hold no protection for her. She stated, "You cannot hurt anyone by telling the truth, and no one can hurt you by telling a lie."

The next friends tried to require Eddy's appearance in the courtroom but the judge instead appointed three men to visit Eddy to determine her competence. They interviewed her on August 14, accompanied by Chandler and a court stenographer. Upon their arrival, one told Eddy to let them know if at any time during the interview she felt fatigued.

Eddy replied, "I can work hours at my work, day and night, without fatigue when it is in this line of thought." She then responded to a series of questions about her past, her investment philosophy, and her religion.

As the inquirers left, Chandler was overheard to say that Eddy was "smarter than a steel trap." Because Eddy proved she was more than capable of conducting her own affairs, the suit fell apart. She successfully appointed trustees to care for her personal finances, relieving her of further obligations. Eddy made a pointed observation at the dismissal of the suit. "If I were a man," she said, "they would not treat me so."

During and after the suit, Eddy was busy writing letters about a proposed edition of *Science and Health* in German, among other projects. Her work continued unabated, and much as she loved Pleasant View, she felt it necessary to move on to accomplish new goals. She instructed her

An informal snapshot of members of Eddy's household at Chestnut Hill shows them cheerfully sitting down to dinner. Although they were mindful of the demands of serving there, they recalled the time they spent learning and living Christian Science at Chestnut Hill with gratitude.

household to find a new estate for her in Massachusetts, outside Boston. They did so, but the keen scrutiny of the press presented unusual problems during the move.

On January 26, 1908, a special train arranged in secrecy met Eddy in Concord. To avoid reporters or crowds, Eddy left Concord unannounced. The train departed toward Boston with an extra engine, to protect it from any possible mishap.

The caravan veered off to a small station in Chestnut Hill, where a fleet of empty carriages met Eddy and her entourage. Despite the group's precautions, however, numerous reporters lay in wait at Eddy's destination. When the carriages rode up to the gates, a friend scooped Eddy into his arms, carried her past the reporters, and set her down laughing in her new home. Although the gallant action amused her, Peel reported that when she had settled in her room, she wept — shocked at the size and expense of the 25-room mansion her students had chosen.

Eddy sought a more peaceful atmosphere after the next friends suit but still, at the age of 87, she was not ready for complete retirement. In July she took what she is reported to have later called "the greatest step forward since I gave *Science and Health* to the world." She wrote to the Board of Directors:

> *Notice.* So soon as the Pub. House debt is paid I request The C. S. Board [of] Directors to start a daily newspaper called *Christian Science Monitor*. This must be *done* without fail.

The board was taken aback by the request, as Peel noted, for they had just finished arranging for new facilities to be built to house the existing publishing operations. They suggested to Eddy that the orders should go to the trustees of the Publishing Society, stalling for time.

In August, the Publishing Society moved into its new debt-free headquarters, and Eddy promptly directed her order to the trustees: "Let there be no delay. The Cause demands that it be issued now."

Eddy planned the newspaper, in part, as a counterpoint to the many low-quality, sensationalist newspapers of the day. Newspapers such as William Randolph Hearst's *New York Evening Journal* had been partially responsible for instigating the Spanish-American War and generally were filled with lurid stories. The *Monitor* was not to be primarily concerned with news of the Christian Science movement. Its first editor, Archibald McLellan, said it was intended to be a "real newspaper."

In order to produce a brand-new daily, the just-finished publishing house required immediate expansion and new machinery. The ranks of Christian Scientists were combed for reputable, experienced journalists who could join the staff. Editorial and business procedures were quickly devised.

Some Christian Scientists feared the prospective name would discourage non-Scientists from reading the paper. Finally, McLellan visited Eddy to convince her the newspaper would reach more people without the words *Christian Science* in its title. When McLellan exited he said, "Mrs. Eddy is firm and her answer is 'God gave me this name and it remains.'"

After only 3½ months, the first 12-page issue of *The Christian Science Monitor* appeared on November 25. The editors and writers of the *Monitor* strove to inform all citizens accurately about events of the day and, in Eddy's words, to "injure no man, but to bless all mankind." It contained "strictly up-to-date" news of the world and one daily religious article. Eddy saw it as a paper with a purpose, rather than merely a popular daily.

Meanwhile, Eddy continued to expand the *Manual of The Mother Church,* readying it to guide her church when she was no longer there. "Many times a single By-law has cost me long nights of prayer and struggle," she once wrote to the Board of Directors. "Never abandon the By-laws nor the denominational government of the Mother Church. If I am not personally with you, the Word of God, and my instructions in the By-laws have led you hitherto and will remain to guide you safely on."

Increasingly, she refused to answer requests from the Board of Directors to make important church decisions, encouraging them to turn directly to God for guidance. In November 1909, she declared in the *Journal,* "I hereby publicly declare that I am not personally involved in the affairs of the church in any other way than through my written and published rules."

The pace of daily life at the house in Chestnut Hill visibly slowed and relaxed, as Peel noted from recollections of household members. Eddy wrote and dictated less, got up later, and spent more time on her daily drive. After her evening meal, she enjoyed watching the stars come out beyond her front yard. A Victrola was installed in the parlor, and members of the household frequently gave singing recitals or joined in group song. Yet, she still remained involved enough to name a new director to the board to replace one who died in November.

On December 1, 1910, suffering from a severe cold, Eddy went out for her carriage ride. Upon her return, she had to be carried upstairs, where she asked for paper. She wrote

The domed extension of The Mother Church majestically rises next to the original church (visible on the right) in the Back Bay section of Boston. Visitors from all over the world come to admire the church's architecture and see the center of the worldwide Christian Science organization. They may also visit the home of The Christian Science Publishing Society (the building to the right of the church), where *The Christian Science Monitor* is edited and other periodicals are edited and printed. This building also houses a 30-foot stained-glass globe called the Mapparium, which attracts many sightseers.

her last words, "God is my life." Two days later, she died quietly.

The next morning the first reader in The Mother Church ended the Sunday service with the following words:

"I shall now read part of a letter written by our revered Leader and reprinted on page 135 of 'Miscellaneous Writings:'

'MY BELOVED STUDENTS: — You may be looking to see me in my accustomed place with you, but this you must no longer expect. When I retired from the field of labor, it was a departure, socially, publicly, and finally, from the routine of such material modes as society and our societies demand. Rumors are rumors, — nothing more. I am still with you on the field of battle, taking forward marches, broader and higher views, and with the hope that you will follow. . . . All our thoughts should be given to the absolute demonstration of Christian Science. You can well afford to give me up, since you have in my last revised edition of Science and Health your teacher and guide.'

"Although these lines were written years ago, they are true to-day, and will continue to be true. But it has now become my duty to announce that Mrs. Eddy passed from our sight last night at 10:45 o'clock, at her home in Chestnut Hill."

During Eddy's earlier days in Boston, when clergy criticized her mercilessly, many claimed that Christian Science would die when she died. By 1990, approximately 1,850 branch churches existed in the United States alone. As of 1990, Christian Science congregations existed in more than 60 countries, and Eddy's writings have been translated into 16 languages. *Science and Health* has broken all publishing and printing records for religious books other than the Bible. *The Christian Science Monitor* is widely read and has

Eddy's achievement as an American woman who founded
a vital, successful international religion is immensely impressive,
but she deemed her discovery of truth and spiritual
healing and her communication of it to the world to be
far more important than material success.

maintained a fine reputation as a major international newspaper. In recent years the *Monitor* has expanded its publishing activities into local, national, and international broadcasting on both radio and television.

Without a doubt Eddy achieved her childhood ambition, for when she boldly asserted, "I want to write a book," she did not dream that someday in more than 60 nations around the world people would organize Christian Science branch churches and societies. Nor could she have dreamed that her writing and teaching would become the basis for a church and a ministry of spiritual healing. Perhaps her true achievement can be measured best by understanding her own evaluation of herself: "What I am remains to be proved by the good I do."

Chronology

July 16, 1821 Born Mary Morse Baker in Bow, New Hampshire

1836 Baker family moves to farm near Sanbornton Bridge, New Hampshire

1842 Mary Baker attends Sanbornton Academy at Sanbornton Bridge

1843 Marries George Washington Glover

1844 Glover dies; Mary returns to Sanbornton Bridge farm; a son, George Washington Glover II, born on September 12

1851 George Glover moves to live with Mahala and Russell Cheney

1853 Mary Glover marries Dr. Daniel Patterson

1862 Receives treatment from Phineas P. Quimby in Portland, Maine

1866 Seriously injured by fall on ice; healed at home in Swampscott, Massachusetts; Pattersons move to Clark boardinghouse in Lynn, Massachusetts, where Dr. Patterson deserts his wife

1866–68 Mary Patterson moves many times; works on writings

1870 Returns to Lynn; remains there for next 12 years

1873 Divorces Patterson

1875 Buys house at 8 Broad Street, Lynn; publishes *Science and Health*

1876 Organizes Christian Scientist Association

1877 Marries Asa Gilbert Eddy

1879 Forms Church of Christ, Scientist

135

1881 Massachusetts Metaphysical College chartered

1882 Gilbert Eddy dies

1883 First issue of *Journal of Christian Science* appears

1888 Eddy delivers speech at Central Music Hall, Chicago; adopts Ebenezer J. Foster

1889 Gives *Journal* to National Christian Scientist Association; moves to Concord, New Hampshire; Christian Scientist Association and Massachusetts Metaphysical College dissolved; church formally disorganized

1891 Publishes major revision (50th) of *Science and Health with Key to the Scriptures*

1892 Eddy moves to Pleasant View, New Hampshire; The Mother Church is formally reorganized

1894 Eddy names the Bible and *Science and Health* as pastor of the Church of Christ, Scientist

1895 Church building dedicated; Eddy publishes *Manual of The Mother Church*

1898 Founds Board of Lectureship and The Christian Science Publishing Society; first Christian Science church in Germany organized at Hannover; first issue of the *Christian Science Weekly* (renamed *Sentinel*) appears; Eddy teaches last class at Concord

1902 Publishes last major revision of *Science and Health;* church membership pledges $2 million toward a new and enlarged edifice

1903 Publishes the first foreign-language periodical, *The Herald of Christian Science,* for the German Christian Scientists

1906 Dedication of new church edifice for The Mother Church; *New York World* and *McClure's* magazine publish articles attacking Eddy

1907 William Chandler begins next friends suit; masters' interview at Pleasant View; failure of next friends suit; Eddy vindicated

1908 Moves from Pleasant View to Chestnut Hill, Massachusetts; first issue of *The Christian Science Monitor* appears

Dec. 3, 1910 Dies at home in Chestnut Hill

Index